WOOD®
SHOP-TESTED
OUTDOOR FURNITURE
YOU CAN MAKE

WE CARE!

All of us at Meredith® Books are dedicated to giving you the
information and ideas you need to create beautiful and useful
woodworking projects. We guarantee your satisfaction with this
book for as long as you own it. We also welcome your comments
and suggestions. Please write us at Meredith® Books, RW 240,
1716 Locust St., Des Moines, IA 50309-3023.

A **WOOD**® **BOOK**
An imprint of Meredith® Books

SHOP-TESTED OUTDOOR FURNITURE YOU CAN MAKE
Hardcover Edition
Produced by Roundtable Press, Inc.
Directors: Susan E. Meyer, Marsha Melnick
Senior Editor: Sue Heinemann
Managing Editor: Ross L. Horowitz
Graphic Designer: Leah Lococo
Design Assistant: Leslie Goldman
Art Assistant: Ahmad Mallah
Copy Assistant: Amy Handy

Meredith® Books
Editorial Project Manager/Assistant Art Director: Tom Wegner
Contributing How-To Editor: Marlen Kemmet
Contributing How-To Editor: Charles E. Sommers
Contributing Tool Editor: Larry Johnston
Contributing Outline Editor: David A. Kirchner

Special thanks to Khristy Benoit

Tradepaper Edition
Editor: Benjamin W. Allen
Contributing Editors: Marlen Kemmet, Lisa Green
Cover Illustration: Michael Halbert

Meredith® Books
Editor in Chief: James D. Blume
Design Director: Matt Strelecki
Managing Editor: Gregory H. Kayko
Vice President, General Manager: Jamie L. Martin

WOOD® **Magazine**
Editor: Larry Clayton

Meredith Publishing Group
President, Publishing Group: Christopher M. Little
Vice President and Publishing Director: John P. Loughlin

Meredith Corporation
Chairman of the Board: Jack D. Rehm
President and Chief Executive Officer: William T. Kerr
Chairman of the Executive Committee: E.T. Meredith III

Note to the Reader: Due to differing conditions, tools, and individual skills, Meredith Corporation assumes no responsibility for any damages, injuries suffered, or losses incurred as a result of following the information published in this book. Before beginning any project, review the instructions carefully, and if any doubts or questions remain, consult local experts or authorities. Because codes and regulations vary greatly, you always should check with authorities to ensure that your project complies with all applicable local codes and regulations. Always read and observe all of the safety precautions provided by any tool or equipment manufacturer, and follow all accepted safety procedures.

C'MON AND SIT
A SPELL

If you want a place to relax on your porch or patio, build the swing, rocker, or outdoor chairs described here. To help you entertain outside, there are also plans for a mahogany table and a folding snack table.

LAZY-DAYS PORCH SWING

Offering plenty of room for two adults to relax and carry on small talk, this inviting project may be the best seat at your house this summer. Made of sturdy oak, our comfortable swing measures over 58" wide and hangs from a pair of chains.

Note: Because of space limitations, we can't provide full-sized patterns for this project. However, to enable you to build the project, we've included gridded patterns. To enlarge these patterns, see the instructions on page 96.

First, make the support pieces

1. Rip and crosscut three pieces of 1⅟₁₆" oak stock to 4¼×22" for the seat supports (A). (See the Cutting Diagram on *page 9*.) For the back supports (B), rip and crosscut three 3¼×24" pieces.

2. Using the Swing Support drawing and the full-sized patterns for reference, mark the location of the half lap joint on the end of each seat support (A) and back support (B).

3. Mount a ¾"-wide dado on your tablesaw. Elevate the dado blade to cut exactly half the thickness of your stock. (We used scrap of the same thickness as the supports and made test cuts to verify the blade height.) Place the miter gauge in the table's slot, and angle it 25° from center. Cut a half lap on one end of each of the three seat support pieces (A) back and support ends (B) where shown in the drawing *right center.*

4. Dry-clamp the three supports (one A and one B per support) to check the fit. Glue and clamp the parts (A, B). (We used slow-set epoxy; you could also use Titebond II water-resistant glue or resorcinol glue.) If you use epoxy, slip on vinyl gloves, and immediately wipe off excess epoxy with a clean cloth dampened with acetone. Acetone will remove uncured epoxy.

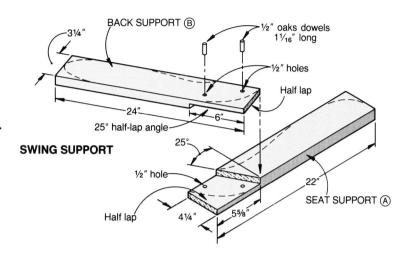

SWING SUPPORT

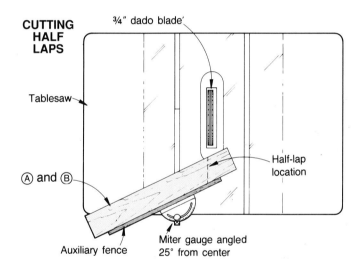

CUTTING HALF LAPS

5. With a scissors, cut the full-sized seat-support and back-support patterns to shape. Tape the patterns together, and then position the taped-together pattern on one of the swing support assemblies. Trace the outline of the seat and back support onto the assembly. Use an awl to make an indentation at each dowel centerpoint. Trace the swing-support pattern onto the other two assembled supports.

6. Drill two ½" holes for the dowels in each support. Cut six 1⅛" lengths of ½" dowel. Glue a dowel in each hole. Drill a ⅜" hole ⅜" deep near the front edge on the *inside* face of the two outside supports where shown on the full-sized pattern.

7. Using a bandsaw or jigsaw, cut the swing support assemblies to shape, cutting just outside the marked lines. Then, use double-faced tape to adhere the three supports face-to-face with the edges flush. Using a drum sander or the rounded end of a portable or stationary sander, sand to the marked line to finish shaping the assemblies. This ensures all three supports are the same shape. Pry the pieces apart, remove the double-faced tape, and then finish-sand each support.

continued

LAZY-DAYS PORCH SWING
continued

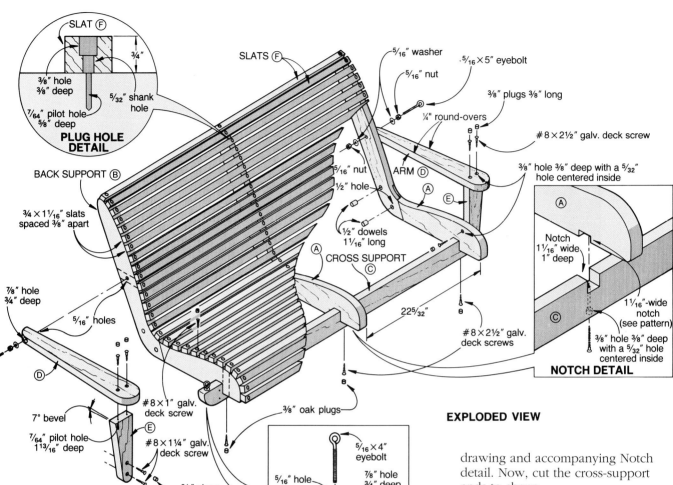

PLUG HOLE DETAIL

SLAT (F)

¾"

⅜" hole
⅜" deep

⁵⁄₃₂" shank hole

⁷⁄₆₄" pilot hole
⅝" deep

SLATS (F)

⁵⁄₁₆" washer
⁵⁄₁₆" nut
.⁵⁄₁₆ × 5" eyebolt
⅜" plugs ⅜" long

BACK SUPPORT (B)

¾ × 1¹⁄₁₆" slats spaced ⅜" apart

⅞" hole
¾" deep

⁵⁄₁₆" holes

¼" round-overs

⁵⁄₁₆" nut
½" hole

ARM (D)

(A)
(E)

½" dowels 1¹⁄₁₆" long

#8 × 2½" galv. deck screw

⅜" hole ⅜" deep with a ⁵⁄₃₂" hole centered inside

(A)

Notch 1¹⁄₁₆" wide 1" deep

(A)

(C)

1¹⁄₁₆"-wide notch (see pattern)

⅜" hole ⅜" deep with a ⁵⁄₃₂" hole centered inside

NOTCH DETAIL

(A)

CROSS SUPPORT (C)

22⁵⁄₃₂"

#8 × 2½" galv. deck screws

7° bevel

⁷⁄₆₄" pilot hole 1¹³⁄₁₆" deep

(D)

#8 × 1" galv. deck screw

(E)

#8 × 1¼" galv. deck screw

⅜" plugs ⅜" long

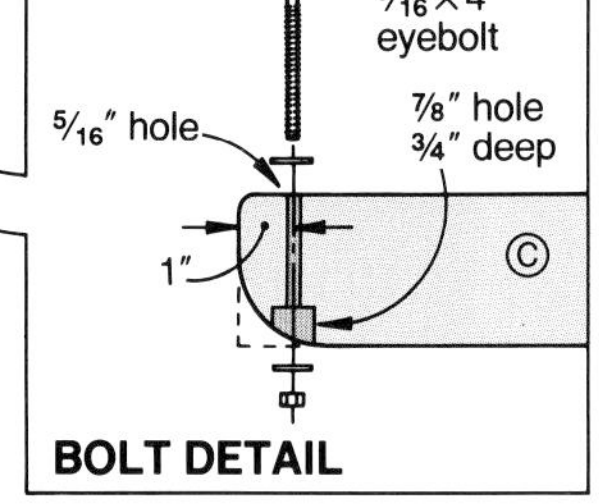

⅜" oak plugs

EXPLODED VIEW

⁵⁄₁₆ × 4" eyebolt

⁵⁄₁₆" hole

⅞" hole ¾" deep

1"

(C)

BOLT DETAIL

Bill of Materials

Part	Finished Size*			Mat.	Qty.
	T	W	L		
A* seat sup.	1¹⁄₁₆"	4¼"	21¼"	WO	3
B* back sup.	1¹⁄₁₆"	3¼"	23½"	WO	3
C cross sup.	1¹⁄₁₆"	3"	58½"	WO	1
D* arms	1¹⁄₁₆"	3"	24½"	WO	2
E* arm sup.	1¹⁄₁₆"	3"	12¾"	WO	2
F seat slats	1¹⁄₁₆"	¾"	47½"	WO	28

*Initially cut parts marked with an * oversized. Then, trim each to finished size according to the how-to instructions.

Material Key: WO–White Oak.
Supplies: 2–⁵⁄₁₆×5" eyebolts, 2–⁵⁄₁₆×4" eye bolts, 6–⁵⁄₁₆" nuts, 8–⁵⁄₁₆" flat washers, #8×1" galvanized deck screws, #8X1¼" galvanized deck screws, #8X2½" galvanized deck screws, ½" oak dowel, 210 passing link zinc chain, 4–lap or quick links.

8. For the cross support (C), rip and crosscut a piece of 1¹⁄₁₆" oak to 3×58½". With your drill press, drill the bolt hole at each end of the cross support, using the dimensions in the Bolt Detail accompanying the Exploded View drawing *above*. Now, finish-sand the piece.

9. Transfer the full-sized Cross-Support End pattern onto the left end of the cross support (C), and mark the end's shape and the notch on the piece. Flip the pattern, and mark the opposite end of the cross support the same way. Locate and mark the center notch where shown on the Exploded View

drawing and accompanying Notch detail. Now, cut the cross-support ends to shape.

10. Cut the three 1¹⁄₁₆"-wide and 1" deep notches in the cross support. (We notched the piece on our tablesaw, using a miter gauge and dado blade, and cleaned the bottoms with a wood chisel.)

11. Angle the dado blade in your tablesaw 7° from perpendicular, and set the blade height (1¹⁄₁₆" maximum as indicated on the pattern), and using the miter gauge for support, cut the 1¹⁄₁₆" notches in the bottom edge of the seat supports as shown *opposite, top.* Clean the notch bottoms with a chisel.

Now, make the arms, arm supports, and the seat supports

1. Cut the full-sized arm (D) and arm-support (E) patterns to shape.

2. From 1¹⁄₁₆"-thick oak, rip and crosscut two pieces to 3¼×25" for the arms (D), and two pieces to 3¼"X13" for the arm supports (E).

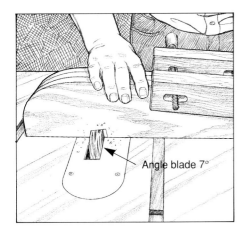

Angle blade 7°

Set the arm-support pieces aside temporarily. Trace the arm pattern outline onto the arm pieces (we labeled them top *left* and top *right*), and mark the centerpoints for the screw holes and the centerline for the ⁵⁄₁₆" horizontal bolt hole. Bandsaw the arms to shape, and sand the edges. (We taped the identical pieces together top face to top face using double-faced tape, and then sanded them with our disc sander.)

3. With a try square, extend the bolt's centerline down the edge of each arm piece, and then find the centers on each edge and mark. Separate the pieces and remove the tape. Turn one of the arms on edge, and with a spade bit or Forstner bit, bore a ⅞"-diameter hole ¾" deep. (We held the arm in a handscrew clamp, and then clamped that assembly to the drill-press table for drilling.) Bore the other arm. Switch to a ⁵⁄₁₆" bit, center it in the ⅞" hole, and drill through the arm. (When drilling, we placed scrap under the arm to avoid chip-out.) Drill the second arm the same way.

4. Rout a ¼" round-over along the top edge of both arms, routing where marked on the full-sized arm pattern.

5. Using double-faced tape, stick the two arm-support pieces together. Trace the arm-support pattern on the top of one piece. Bandsaw the pieces to shape and sand the edges. Separate the pieces, and finish-sand the surfaces on the arm and arm-support pieces.

How we chose the wood and fasteners for our swing

After weighing the merits of several types of lumber for this project, we selected white oak. Native to the eastern United States and Canada, white oak rates as one of the heaviest, strongest, and hardest of all the oaks. The pores of this species contain tyloses—bubblelike structures that form in the vessels of certain hardwoods and resist liquids from penetrating. This attribute makes white oak a perfect material for liquid containers and barrels, and an excellent candidate for outdoor furniture such as our porch swing.

If you have trouble locating white oak, you could substitute redwood or cedar. Or, if you wish to cut costs, you could use fir or pine pressure-treated deck material. You'll need to plane the treated stock to the thickness listed in the Bill of Materials.

What are the best fasteners to use in this case? We recommend either stainless-steel or galvanized deck and machine screws. The tannic acid in white oak along with Mother Nature causes ordinary screws to rust and discolor the wood.

For the adhesive, we recommend Titebond II water-resistant glue, slow-set epoxy, or resorcinol glue to stand up to the wrath of the great outdoors.

6. Lay out one *left* and one *right* arm support and position the screw hole centerpoints accordingly. Drill and counterbore the ⅜" screw holes ⅜" deep in the arm and arm-support parts. Using your tablesaw, cut a 7° bevel on the flat or top end of each arm support. (See the Exploded View drawing for reference. To correctly orient the supports, place the straight sides up against the seat supports, and angle the bevels toward the back of the swing.)

7. From 1¹⁄₁₆"-thick oak, cut 28 seat slats (F) to ¾ ×47½". Sand a slight round-over along the top edges and ends of each slat.

8. Drill three counterbored screw holes in each slat where dimensioned in the Plug Hole detail accompanying the Exploded View drawing. (We set up a fence and a stopblock to consistently position the slats when drilling the mounting holes.)

You're ready to assemble the swing

1. Place the assembled swing supports over the edge of a bench or table so the backs point toward the floor. Place the cross support over the seat supports and engage the mating notches. Once in place, drill the ⅜" counterbore ⅜" deep and ⁵⁄₃₂" shank holes through the cross supports and ⁷⁄₆₄" pilot holes into the seat supports. (For this we used a portable electric drill.) Apply epoxy or resorcinol glue to the mating areas, and then drive a #8×2½" galvanized deck screw in each hole. (See the Notch Detail for reference.)

2. Place a 4×8' sheet of ¾" plywood on your bench or table. Rip and crosscut a 54"-long piece of 1×4" pine or fir and screw it to the front edge of the plywood. Next, lay one of the seat slats against the 1×4 and clamp stopblocks at both ends. Remove the slat and place the assembly from the previous step on top of the plywood. Align the tips of the seat supports so they center between the stopblocks and against the 1×4 as shown on *page 8, top left*. Square the seat supports to the cross support.

3. Position three scrap blocks against the seat supports at the back and screw them to the plywood base. Clamp the supports to these blocks.

continued

LAZY-DAYS PORCH SWING
continued

4. Place the first seat slat on the top edge of the 1×4, align it with the end supports, and then glue and screw it to the supports. (We drilled ⁷⁄₆₄" pilot holes into the supports before driving the #8×1" galvanized deck screws.)

5. Build a pair of spacers like those shown in the drawing at *right.*

6. Lay the second slat in place, using the spacers to position it ⅜" away from the first. Attach the slat like you did the first one. As shown in the drawing *below bottom,* glue and screw the remaining slats to the supports, using the spacers to maintain the ⅜" spacing.

7. Glue and screw the arm supports to the cross support. (We applied glue, placed the straight side of the supports against the

Blocks screwed to plywood

1×4×54" strip

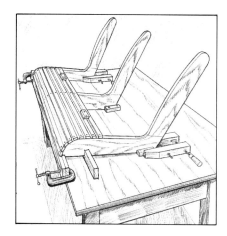

seat supports with the bevel pointing down toward the back of the swing, aligned the parts at the bottom, and then clamped them in place. Next, we drilled ⁷⁄₆₄" pilot holes into the cross support, and drove #8×1¼" deck screws.) Drive a #8×2½" galvanized deck screw through each of the outside seat supports and into the arm supports.

8. Position the right arm on the arm support, center the screw holes, and then temporarily clamp the back end of the arm to the back support so the arm sits squarely on the arm support's beveled edge. Drill ⁷⁄₆₄" pilot holes (through the arm holes) into the arm supports. Drive one screw to temporarily hold the arm. Switch to a ⁵⁄₁₆" bit, place it in the hole in the end of the arm, and drill a hole through the back support. Remove the arm from the assembly.

9. Assemble the eyebolt as shown on the Exploded View drawing, and insert it through the arm. Apply glue to the mating parts on the arm, arm support, and back supports. Insert the eyebolt through the back support, add a washer, and then the second nut. Drive the two screws through the arm and into the arm support. Tighten the nut on the eyebolt. Attach the other arm the same way.

10. Attach the eyebolts in the ends of the cross support as shown in the Bolt Detail on the Exploded View drawing.

11. Using a ⅜" plug cutter, cut 97 plugs from scrap ⁷⁄₁₆" oak (we planed thick stock to size). Glue the plugs in the counterbored screw holes so the grain of the plug aligns with the grain of the slats. Sand the plugs flush with the surrounding surface.

12. Apply the finish of your choice. (Because the swing will be used outdoors, we applied two coats of Flood Clear Wood Finish, an oil-based wood preservative. This product applies easily, and can

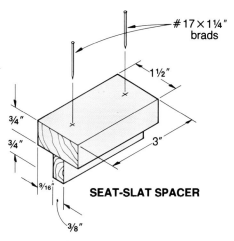

#17×1¼"
brads

1½"

¾"

¾"

3"

9⁄16"

3⁄8"

SEAT-SLAT SPACER

be reapplied as needed without much surface preparation.)

13. Attach the chain to the eyebolts (use either S-hooks, lap links, or quick links—available where you buy the chain), and hang the swing. Adjust its height to a comfortable level. Cut the links with a hacksaw to remove unneeded chain. Now, enjoy the fruits of your labor.

Project Tool List
Dado blade or dado set
Bandsaw
Drill press
  Bits: ⁷⁄₆₄", ⁵⁄₃₂", ⁵⁄₁₆", ⅜", ½" ⅞"
  ⅜" plug cutter
Router
  ¼" round-over bit
Belt sander
Finishing sander

Note: We built the project using the tools listed. You may be able to substitute other tools or equipment for listed items you don't have. Additional common hand tools and clamps may be required to complete the project.

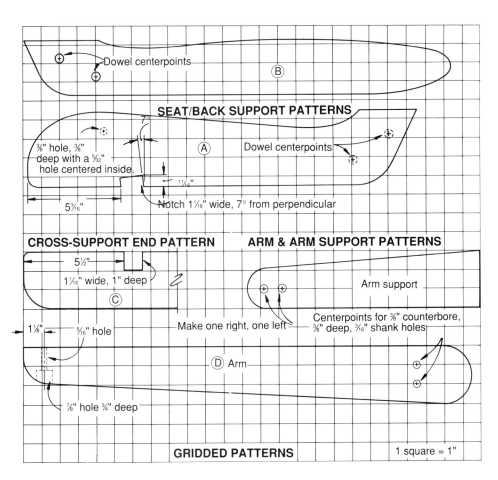

Dowel centerpoints

(B)

SEAT/BACK SUPPORT PATTERNS

³⁄₈" hole, ³⁄₈"
deep with a ⁵⁄₃₂"
hole centered inside.

(A)   Dowel centerpoints

1¹⁄₁₆"

5³⁄₁₆"   Notch 1¹⁄₁₆" wide, 7° from perpendicular

CROSS-SUPPORT END PATTERN   **ARM & ARM SUPPORT PATTERNS**

5½"

1¹⁄₁₆" wide, 1" deep   Arm support

(C)

1⅛"   ⁵⁄₁₆" hole   Make one right, one left   Centerpoints for ³⁄₈" counterbore,
³⁄₈" deep, ³⁄₁₆" shank holes

(D) Arm

⅞" hole ¾" deep

GRIDDED PATTERNS   1 square = 1"

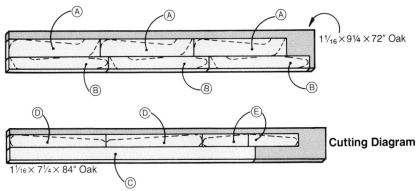

(A)   (A)   (A)

1¹⁄₁₆ × 9¼ × 72″ Oak

(B)   (B)   (B)

(D)   (D)   (E)

Cutting Diagram

1¹⁄₁₆ × 7¼ × 84" Oak

(C)

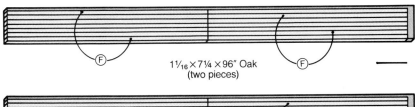

(F)   (F)

1¹⁄₁₆ × 7¼ × 96″ Oak
(two pieces)

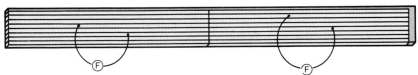

(F)   (F)

LAZY-DAYS PORCH ROCKER

After a hard day's work, what could be more relaxing than sitting back with a tall glass of lemonade in this sturdy, attractive porch rocker? We contoured the seat and back for maximum comfort. For the wood parts, we chose weather-resistant white oak and mahogany so the rocker can be used outdoors.

Note: *Because of space limitations, we can't provide full-sized patterns for this project. However, to enable you to build the project, we've included gridded patterns. To enlarge these patterns, see the instructions on page 96.*

Let's begin with the rocker

1. Cut four pieces of ¾" white oak to 6¼" wide by 32" long for the rocker blanks (A). Plane or resaw each piece to ⅝" thick.

2. Using the dimensions on the Rocker Lamination Drawing *opposite*, mark the dado locations on each rocker blank. Cut the dadoes. (We attached a wooden auxiliary fence to our miter gauge, and clamped a stop to the fence to ensure the dadoes were consistently positioned from blank to blank.)

Note: *For joints that will stand up to the extremes of Mother Nature, use Titebond II water-resistant glue, slow-set epoxy, or resorcinol glue.*

3. Glue the mating rocker blanks (A) face-to-face, with the dadoes aligned and the ends and edges flush. Immediately remove glue squeeze-out from the mortises.

4. Using double-faced (carpet) tape, stick the two rocker blanks together face-to-face, with the edges and ends flush.

5. With a scissors, cut the full-sized rocker pattern to shape. See the Cutting Diagram on *page 12* for how we laid out the patterns. Using spray adhesive, adhere the full-sized rocker pattern to one of the rocker laminations, aligning the dadoes on the pattern with those cut in the wood.

6. Bandsaw the taped-together rocker laminations to shape. Sand the rocker edges flush, sanding to the marked line. Separate the rockers, and remove the tape.

Next, complete the end frame assemblies

1. From 1¹⁄₁₆" Honduras mahogany, cut the legs (B, C) to size. From ¾" mahogany, cut the rails (D) to size.

continued

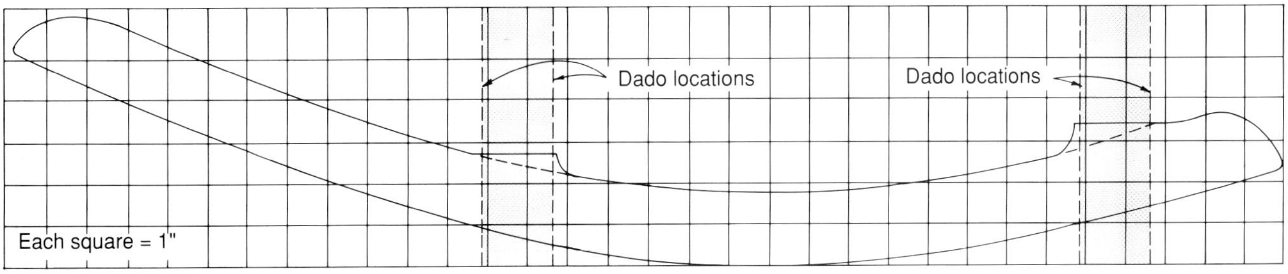
Dado locations
Dado locations
Each square = 1"

ROCKER GRID

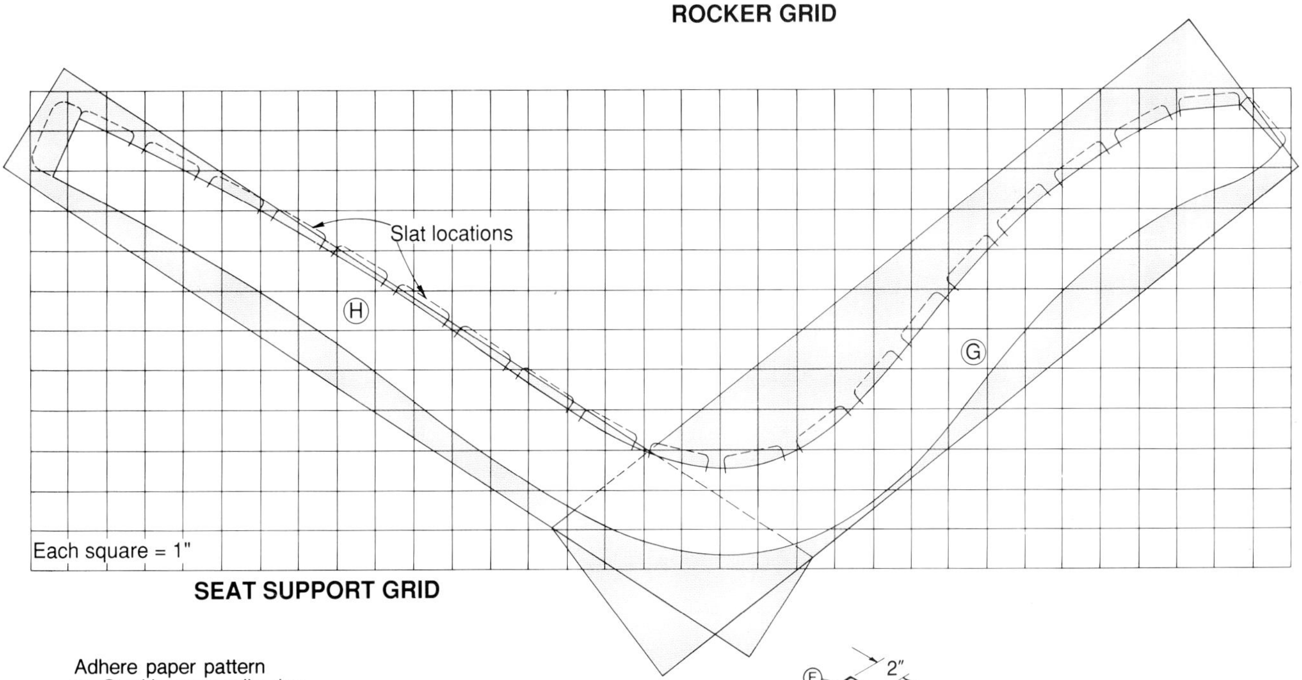
Slat locations
H
G
Each square = 1"

SEAT SUPPORT GRID

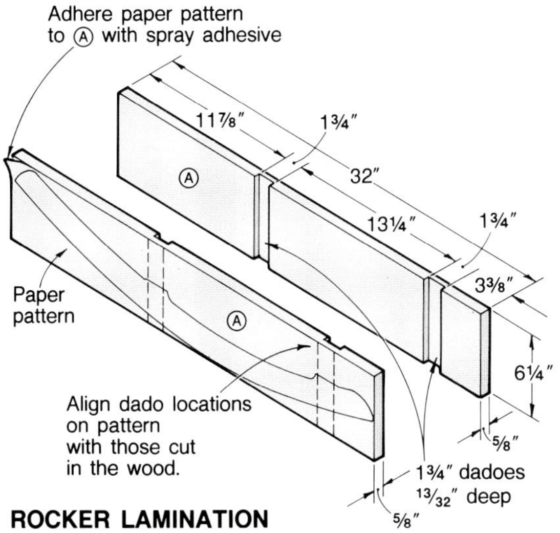
Adhere paper pattern to A with spray adhesive
11⅞″
1¾″
32″
A
13¼″
1¾″
3⅜″
6¼″
Paper pattern
A
Align dado locations on pattern with those cut in the wood.
⅝″
1¾″ dadoes
13/32″ deep
⅝″

ROCKER LAMINATION

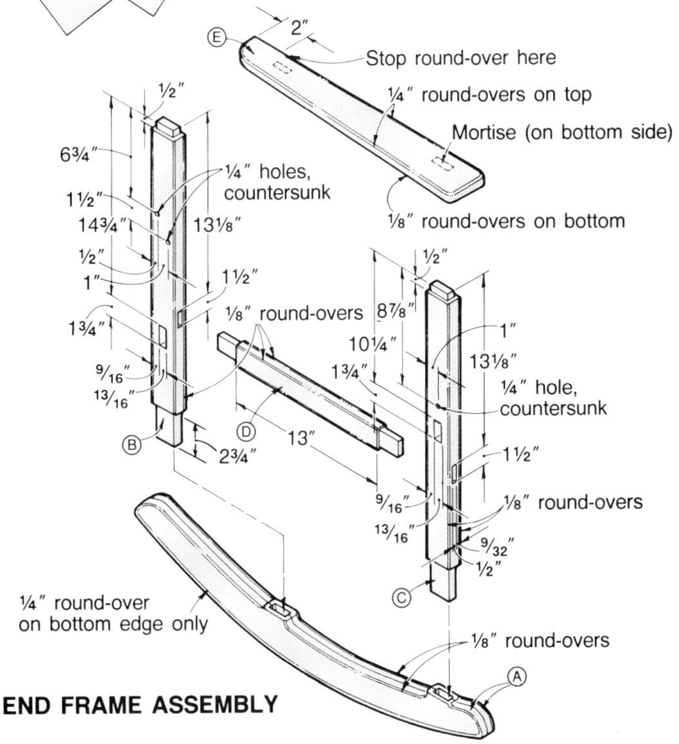
E
2″
Stop round-over here
¼″ round-overs on top
Mortise (on bottom side)
⅛″ round-overs on bottom
½″
6¾″
¼″ holes, countersunk
1½″
14¾″
13⅛″
½″
1″
1½″
⅛″ round-overs
1¾″
9/16″
13/16″
B
2¾″
D
13″
1¾″
½″
8⅞″
10¼″
1″
13⅛″
¼″ hole, countersunk
1½″
⅛″ round-overs
9/16″
13/16″
9/32″
½″
C
¼″ round-over on bottom edge only
⅛″ round-overs
A

END FRAME ASSEMBLY

LAZY-DAYS PORCH ROCKER

continued

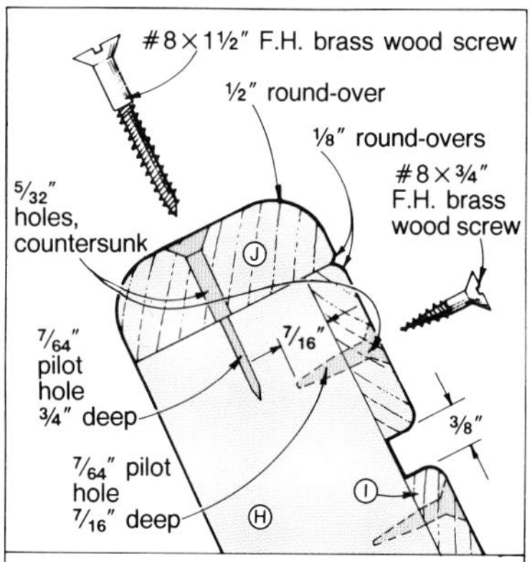
#8 × 1½" F.H. brass wood screw
½" round-over
⅛" round-overs
#8 × ¾" F.H. brass wood screw
5/32" holes, countersunk
7/64" pilot hole ¾" deep
7/16"
⅜"
7/64" pilot hole 7/16" deep
J
H
I

SCREW HOLE DETAIL

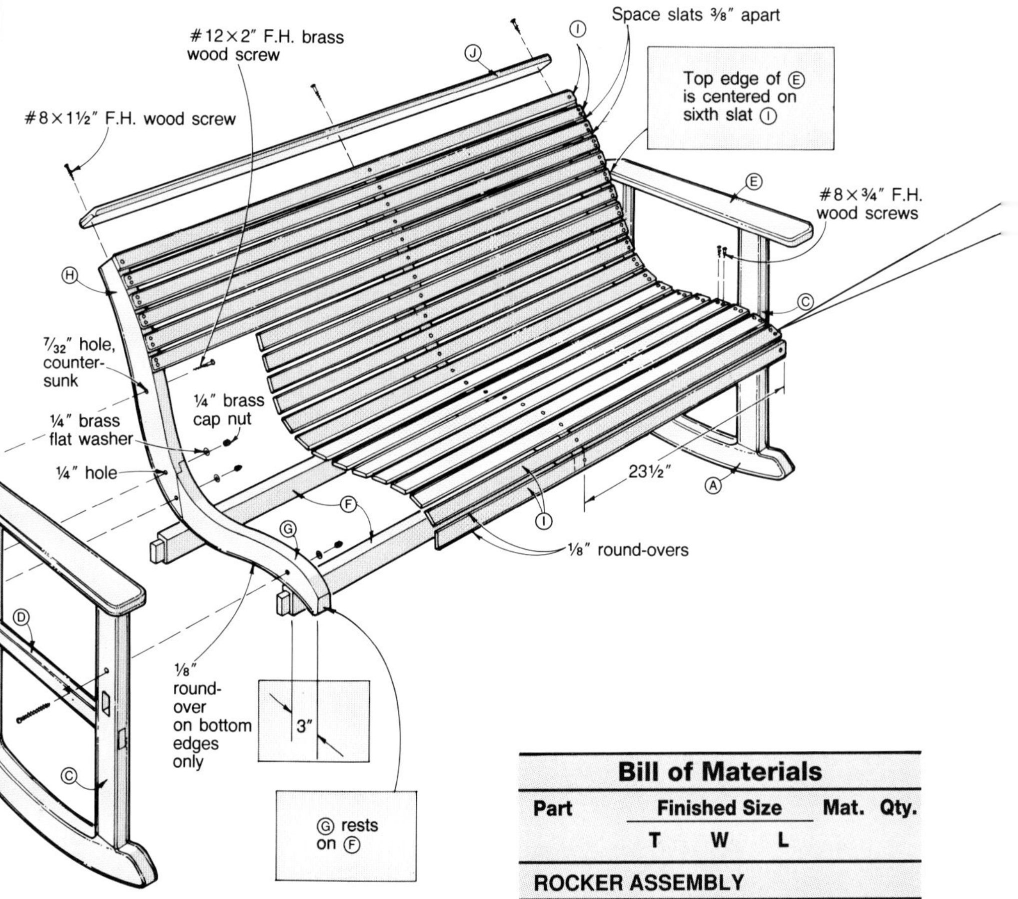
#12 × 2" F.H. brass wood screw
#8 × 1½" F.H. wood screw
Space slats ⅜" apart
Top edge of E is centered on sixth slat I
#8 × ¾" F.H. wood screws
7/32" hole, countersunk
¼" brass flat washer
¼" brass cap nut
¼" hole
Stop round-over here
¼ × 2½" F.H. brass machine screws
23½"
⅛" round-overs
⅛" round-over on bottom edges only
3"
G rests on F

EXPLODED VIEW

CUTTING DIAGRAM

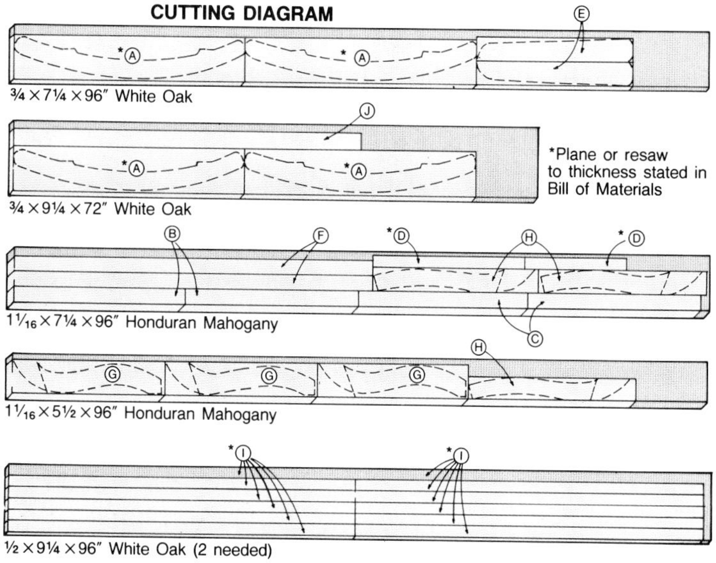
¾ × 7¼ × 96" White Oak
¾ × 9¼ × 72" White Oak
*Plane or resaw to thickness stated in Bill of Materials
1 1/16 × 7¼ × 96" Honduran Mahogany
1 1/16 × 5½ × 96" Honduran Mahogany
½ × 9¼ × 96" White Oak (2 needed)

Bill of Materials

Part	Finished Size T	W	L	Mat.	Qty.
ROCKER ASSEMBLY					
A* rockers	5/8"	6¼"	32"	WO	4
B* back legs	1 1/16"	2"	24 1/16"	HM	2
C* front legs	1 1/16"	2"	23⅜"	HM	2
D rails	¾"	1¾"	17"	HM	2
E armrests	¾"	3¼"	21¼"	WO	2
F stretchers	1 1/16"	2"	50⅛"	HM	2
SEAT ASSEMBLY					
G* btm sup.	1 1/16"	4¾"	21"	HM	3
H* back sup.	1 1/16"	3"	23"	HM	3
I* slats	5/16"	1½"	48"	WO	20
J top slat	¾"	1 15/16"	48"	WO	1

*Dimensions given are initial thickness, length, and width.

Material Key: WO–white oak, HM–Honduras mahogany

Supplies: double-faced tape, spray adhesive, 6–¼X2½" flathead brass machine screws with ¼" brass flat washers and ¼" brass cap nuts, #8X¾" flathead brass wood screws, 3–#8X1½" flathead brass wood screws, 2–#12X2" flathead brass wood screws, clear exterior finish.

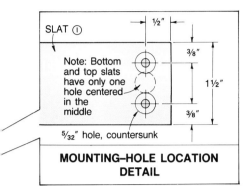

SLAT ①

Note: Bottom and top slats have only one hole centered in the middle

½"
⅜"
1½"
⅜"

5/32" hole, countersunk

MOUNTING–HOLE LOCATION DETAIL

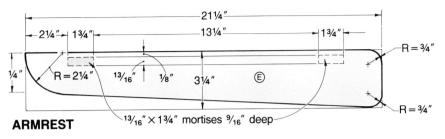

21¼"
2¼" · 1¾"
13¼"
1¾"
R = ¾"
¼"
R = 2¼"
13/16"
⅛"
3¼"
Ⓔ
R = ¾"

13/16" × 1¾" mortises 9/16" deep

ARMREST

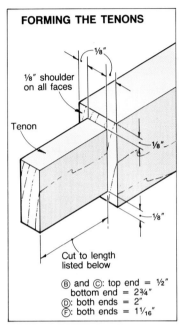

FORMING THE TENONS

⅛"
⅛" shoulder on all faces
Tenon
⅛"
⅛"

Cut to length listed below

Ⓑ and Ⓒ: top end = ½"
bottom end = 2¾"
Ⓓ: both ends = 2"
Ⓕ: both ends = 1¹/₁₆"

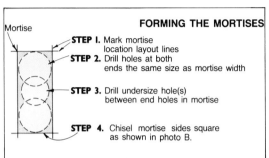

Mortise

FORMING THE MORTISES

STEP 1. Mark mortise location layout lines
STEP 2. Drill holes at both ends the same size as mortise width
STEP 3. Drill undersize hole(s) between end holes in mortise
STEP 4. Chisel mortise sides square as shown in photo B.

A

We used 90° corner braces to hold the rocker frame pieces square while the glue dried.

2. Using the dimensions on the End Frame Assembly drawing on *page 11* and the drawings titled Forming the Mortises and Forming the Tenons at *right,* use a square to mark the mortise, tenon, and hole locations on each leg. Next, mark the tenon locations on each end of the rails.

3. Following the four-step procedure on the drawing at *far right,* form the mortises. Then, cut tenons on the legs and rails.

4. For securing the seat assembly to the end frames later, drill and countersink a pair of ¼" holes in each back leg (B) and one in each front leg (C).

5. Cut two armrest blanks (E) to 3¼×21¼" from ¾"-thick white oak. Using the Armrest drawing for reference, transfer the pattern to one of the pieces. Next, using the method described earlier, tape the armrests together, cut to shape, sand the edges smooth, separate the armrests, and remove the tape.

6. Mark the location for a pair of 9/16"-deep mortises on the bottom of each armrest (E).

7. Rout ⅛" and ¼" round-overs on parts A, B, C, D, and E where shown on the End Frame Assembly and Exploded View drawings.

8. Glue and clamp each end frame assembly, checking for square.

Now, add the stretchers, and join the end assemblies

1. Cut the stretchers (F) to size. Mark and cut 1¹/₁₆"-long tenons on the ends of each stretcher.

2. Glue the pair of stretchers between the end frames as shown in

Photo A. (To ensure that the assembly would stay square, we clamped square corner braces in place and left them there until the glue dried.)

3. Position an armrest on the top of each end assembly, and verify that the marked mortises match the tenon locations on the top of the legs. Re-mark if necessary.

4. Drill overlapping holes 9/16" deep where marked. Then, as shown in Photo B on *page 14,* chisel the mortise sides square, and finish forming the mortise.

5. Glue and clamp an armrest to the top of each end-frame assembly. Immediately wipe off glue squeezed out of the mortise and tenon joints. Later remove the clamps and sand the rocker assembly smooth.

And now for the slat-support assemblies

1. Rip and crosscut three pieces of 1¹/₁₆" mahogany stock to 4¾×21"

for the bottom-slat supports (G) and three pieces to 3×23" for back-slat supports (H).

2. Using the Slat Support drawing on *page 14* for reference, mark the location of the half-lap joint on one end of each slat support (G, H).

3. Mount a ¾"-wide dado blade to your tablesaw. Elevate the blade to cut exactly half the thickness of your stock. (We used scrap the same thickness as the supports, and made test cuts to verify blade height.) Angle the miter gauge 20° from center. Cut a half-lap on one
continued

13

LAZY-DAYS PORCH ROCKER
continued

SLAT SUPPORT

Half-lap joints

5"

3¼"

20°

Note: All dado cuts
are cut at a 20° angle

H

G

Use a mallet and chisel to finish shaping the mortises.

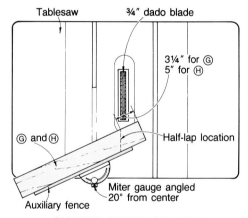

Tablesaw   ¾" dado blade

3¼" for G
5" for H

G and H

Half-lap location

Miter gauge angled
20° from center

Auxiliary fence

CUTTING THE HALF LAPS

end of each of the six slat supports where shown on the drawing *right*.

4. Dry-clamp the three supports (one G and one H per support) to check the fit. Glue and clamp each of the three supports.

5. Following the method described to form the rockers and armrests, tape the supports together, transfer the pattern outlines, cut the supports to shape, and sand the edges. Then, using a try square, transfer the slat (I) locations to the top front edge of each slat support assembly (G, H). Pry the pieces apart, remove the double-faced tape, and finish-sand the supports, being careful not to sand away the slat location lines.

6. Rout ⅛" round-overs along the bottom and back edges of each slat support where shown on the Exploded View drawing.

It's time to fasten the slats to the slat supports

1. From ⁵⁄₁₆"-thick oak (we planed thicker stock to size), cut 20 seat slats (I) to 1½ X48". From ¾" stock, cut the top slat (J) to size.

2. Rout a ⅛" round-over along the top edges and ends of each ⁵⁄₁₆" slat (I) and a ½" round-over along the top edges and ends of the top slat (J). Next, rout a ⅛" round-over along the bottom front edge of the top slat.

3. Drill the countersunk screw holes in each slat where dimensioned on the Exploded View drawing and accompanying Mounting Hole Location detail. (We clamped a fence and a stop-

block to our drill-press table to consistently position the holes from slat to slat.)

4. As shown in the drawing *opposite,* place the three slat supports on your benchtop. Clamp a large handscrew clamp to each to hold the pieces upright.

5. Screw the top slat (J) to the three slat supports. Then, fasten one of the ⁵⁄₁₆" slats (I) to the opposite end of the assembly where shown in the drawing on the Seat Support grid on *page 11*.

6. Following the layout marks on the slat supports, fasten the remaining seat slats (I).

Finishing up

1. With a helper, position the seat assembly on the rocker

SEAT SUPPORT ASSEMBLY

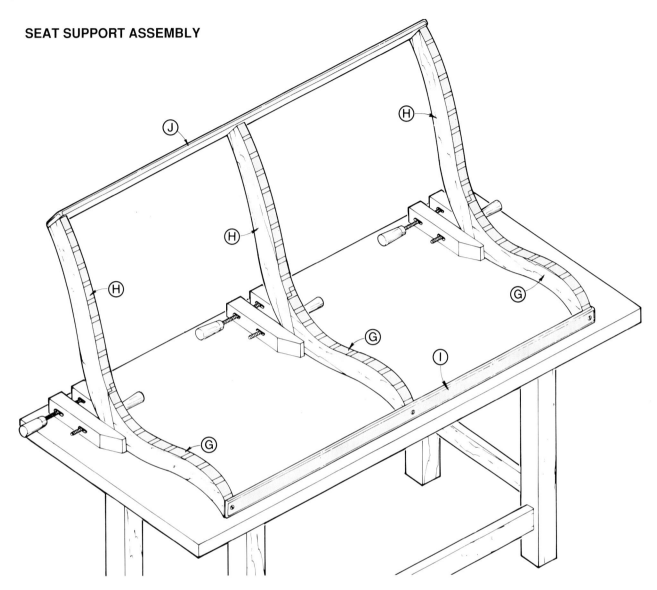

assembly where dimensioned in the tinted boxes on the Exploded View drawing. Once correctly positioned, clamp the seat in place.

2. Using the previously drilled ¼" holes in the front and rear legs as guides, drill ¼" holes through the slat supports. Using ¼" machine screws, fasten the two assemblies.

3. Working from the back inside, drill a ⁷⁄₃₂" shank hole through the back seat support (H) and a ⁵⁄₆₄" pilot hole 1" deep into the inside edge of the armrests. Drive a #12x2" flathead brass wood screw through the support and into the armrest.

4. Remove the screws, and separate the seat assembly from the

rocker assembly. (We found it easier to sand the asemblies when separated.) Finish-sand both assemblies and apply the finish. (We applied three coats of spar varnish.) Later, fasten the two assemblies back together.

Project Tool List
Tablesaw
  Dado blade or dado set
Bandsaw
Portable drill
Drill press
  Bits: ⁷⁄₆₄", ⁵⁄₃₂", ¼", ¹³⁄₁₆"
Router
  ⅛" round-over, ¼" round-over
Belt sander
Finishing sander

Note: *We built the project using the tools listed. You may be able to substitute other tools or equipment for listed items you don't have. Additional common hand tools and clamps may be required to complete the project.*

THE ADIRONDACK LAWN CHAIR

Everyone wants to own a classic, and now you can by taking advantage of one of the most successful chair designs of all time—the super-comfortable Adirondack lawn chair. Our stylish version offers solid wood construction and simple joints.

Note: Because of space limitations, we can't provide full-sized patterns for this project. However, to enable you to build the project, we've included gridded patterns. To enlarge these patterns, see the instructions on page 96.

First, cut the chair pieces

1. To form the chair-back slats, rip and crosscut a piece of 1" pine (¾" actual) to 7x33" (A), a second piece to 5⅞x29", and a third to 5⅞x26½".

2. Mark a 3½" radius on one end of A, and a 2¹⁵⁄₁₆" radius on one end of the other two boards. Using a bandsaw or portable jigsaw, cut the radii on the three boards, then finish-sand edges and surfaces. (We used a palm sander.) Rip the two 5⅞"-wide boards in half to make two B's and two C's.

3. Rip and crosscut the three back support pieces (D, E, F) to the sizes listed in the Bill of Materials. The parts are shown on the Chair Back and Attaching the Chair Back drawings. Then, cut a piece of scrap the same size as D for use later.

4. To form leg/seat supports (G), use double-faced tape to tape together (face-to-face) two pieces of 1x6 measuring at least 37½" long. Trace the leg/seat support pattern onto the top piece, then cut both pieces to shape (we used a bandsaw). Sand the cut edges smooth to remove the saw marks. Separate the pieces, and using the pattern again, mark the seat slat starting point and screw hole centerpoints on both leg/seat supports.

5. Rip and crosscut 13 seat slats (H) to size. Rip bevels on four of the slats as detailed on the Leg/Seat pattern. Also, rip a 25° bevel along one edge of the middle back support (F) where shown on the Screw Hole detail accompanying the Chair Back drawing on *page 18*.

6. To form the front legs (I), crosscut two 1x6 pieces to 19¾" long. Designate one end the top, and place a mark 5½" in from the edge as shown on the Exploded View drawing *opposite*. At the opposite end, mark in 2¼" from the same edge. Draw a line connecting the two marks. Tape the two pieces together and cut them to shape. Next, plane or sand to the line. (We cut the pieces on our bandsaw, then planed the cut edge flat on a jointer.)

7. To shape the arm supports (J), cut two 4x4" squares of ¾"-thick scrap material. From one corner use a compass to draw a 3¼" radius. Then, cut the two pie-shaped arm supports to shape, and sand the bandsawed-radiused edges smooth.

8. Rip and crosscut two pieces of stock to 6¼x28" for the armrests (K). Tape the two pieces together face-to-face, and transfer the full-sized Armrest pattern to the top piece of stock. Cut the armrests to shape. Sand the cut edges, then separate the two. Finally, transfer

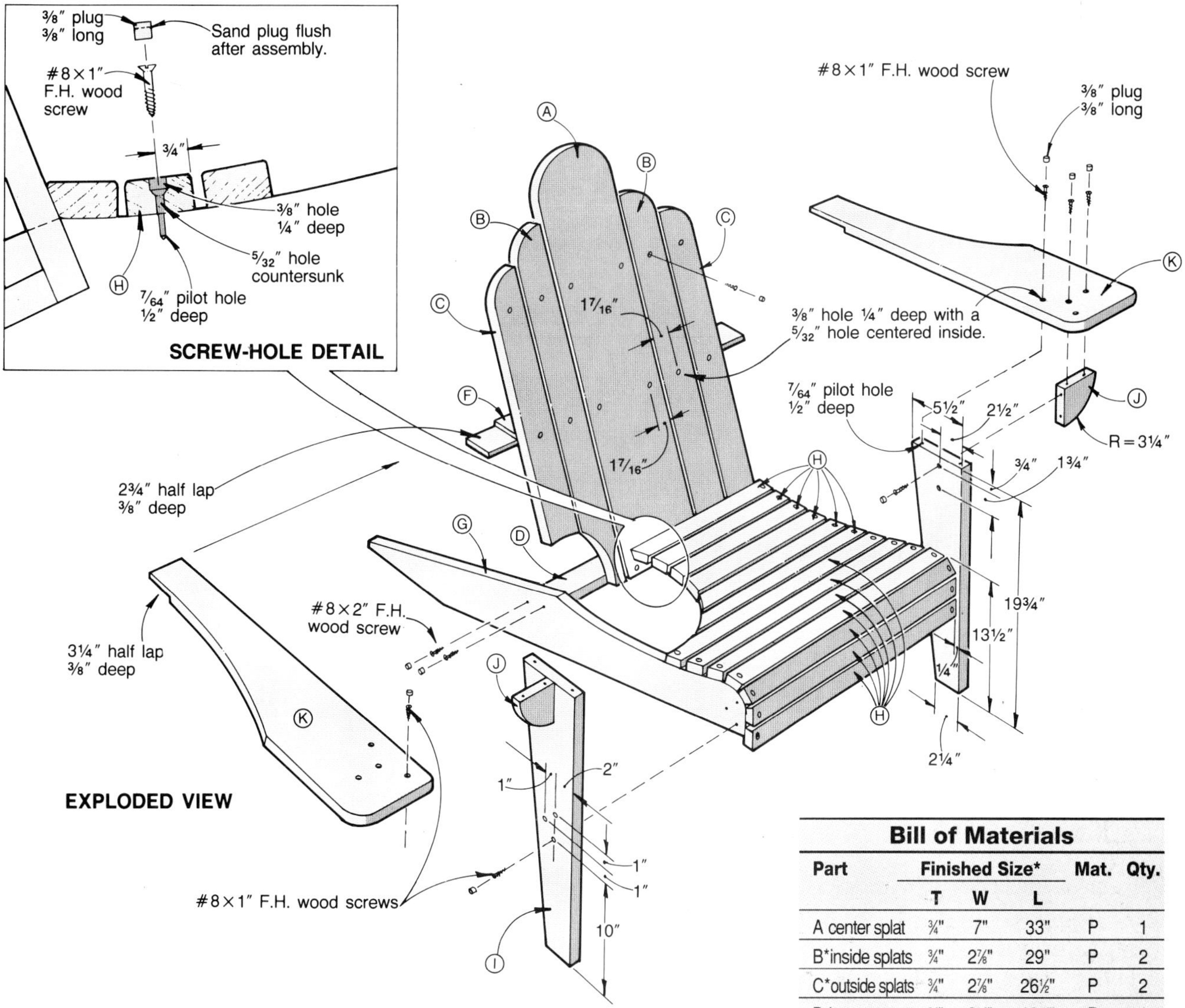

⅜″ plug ⅜″ long
Sand plug flush after assembly.
#8×1″ F.H. wood screw
¾″
⅜″ hole ¼″ deep
5/32″ hole countersunk
7/64″ pilot hole ½″ deep
SCREW-HOLE DETAIL
#8×1″ F.H. wood screw
⅜″ plug ⅜″ long
⅜″ hole ¼″ deep with a 5/32″ hole centered inside.
7/64″ pilot hole ½″ deep
1 7/16″
1 7/16″
5½″
2½″
R=3¼″
¾″
1¾″
19¾″
13½″
¼″
2¼″
2¾″ half lap ⅜″ deep
3¼″ half lap ⅜″ deep
#8×2″ F.H. wood screw
1″
2″
1″
1″
10″
#8×1″ F.H. wood screws
EXPLODED VIEW

Bill of Materials

Part	Finished Size*			Mat.	Qty.
	T	W	L		
A center splat	¾"	7"	33"	P	1
B*inside splats	¾"	2⅞"	29"	P	2
C*outside splats	¾"	2⅞"	26½"	P	2
D lower support	¾"	3½"	19½"	P	1
E top support	¾"	1½"	18½"	P	1
F middle support	¾"	3¼"	25"	P	1
G leg/seat supports	¾"	4 15/16"	37½"	P	2
H slats	¾"	1½"	21"	P	13
I frnt legs	¾"	5½"	19¾"	P	2
J*supports	¾"	3¼"	3¼"	P	2
K armrests	¾"	6¼"	28"	P	2

* Initially cut parts marked with an * oversized. Then trim each to finished size according to the how-to instructions.

Material Key: P–pine
Supplies: ⅜" dowel stock, #8X1" flathead wood screws, #8X2" flat head wood screws, #8X3" galvanized deck screws, exterior paint or finish.

the screw centerpoints from the pattern onto both of the armrests.

9. Cut a 3¼" half lap ⅜" deep across the bottom side of each armrest (K) where shown on the Exploded View drawing and Armrest pattern. Cut a mating half lap across each end of the middle back support piece (F).

Now, counterbore the screw holes

1. Chuck a ⅜" drill bit into your drill press and adjust the stop so it drills ¼" deep in ¾"-thick stock. (We used a brad-point bit.)

2. Lay the backrest splats (A, B, C) good face up on a flat surface and in the order shown in the Exploded View drawing. Align the bottom ends of the splats. On both C's mark points ⅜", 14⅞", and 22⅜" from the bottom ends. With a straightedge, lightly draw lines across all splats connecting the points.

3. Clamp a fence to your drill press table 1 7/16" from the center of the bit. Place either edge of pieces B and C and both edges of piece A against the fence, and drill ⅜" holes ¼" deep centered on the pencil marks. Lay the splats aside for now.

4. To counterbore the seat slats (H), find the center at the end of a slat scrap and drill a ⅜" hole ¼" deep ⅜" in from the end. See the Screw Hole detail accompanying the Exploded View drawing for

continued

THE ADIRONDACK LAWN CHAIR
continued

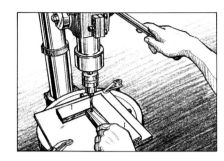

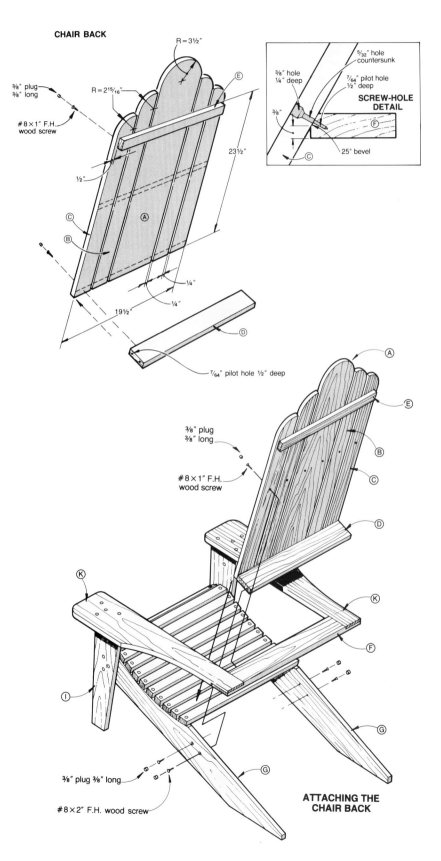

CHAIR BACK

R = 3½"

R = 2¹⁵⁄₁₆"

³⁄₈" plug
³⁄₈" long

#8 × 1" F.H.
wood screw

½"

23½"

¼"

¼"

19½"

⁷⁄₆₄" pilot hole ½" deep

⁵⁄₃₂" hole
countersunk

³⁄₈" hole
¼" deep

⁷⁄₆₄" pilot hole
½" deep

**SCREW-HOLE
DETAIL**

³⁄₈"

25° bevel

³⁄₈" plug
³⁄₈" long

#8 × 1" F.H.
wood screw

³⁄₈" plug ³⁄₈" long

#8 × 2" F.H. wood screw

**ATTACHING THE
CHAIR BACK**

reference. Next, make the right-angle jig shown *above*. Using the scrap piece as a guide, position the jig on the drill-press table, and clamp it in place. Drill the holes.

5. Counterbore the holes in the outside faces of both leg/seat supports (G) where indicated on the pattern. Next, mark center-points on the front legs for the three screw holes located on the outside face and the two on the inside face (see Exploded View drawing). Counterbore those holes in both front legs.

6. Counterbore the holes in the top surface of both armrests, using the dimensions on the Armrest pattern for location.

7. Now, center and drill ⁵⁄₃₂" holes through all of the ⅜" counterbored holes. (We backed the parts with a piece of scrap stock to prevent chip-out.)

It's assembly time

1. Place part D and the same-sized scrap piece you cut earlier on edge about 18" apart on a flat surface. Referring to the Chair Back drawing, lay the backrest splats (A, B, C) across part D. Space the five splats flush with the edge and ends of D. Space the five splats so the back measures 19½" wide. Using a ⁷⁄₆₄" bit and your portable drill, drill a pilot hole through the ⅜" counterbored holes at the bottom of each splat and ½" deep into part D. (See the Screw Hole detail on the Exploded View drawing for details on how all holes are drilled and plugged.) Glue and screw the backrest splats to part D.

2. Draw a line across the back of the backrest 23½" up from the bottom and make a mark ½" in from both edges. Position the top edge of part E on the line, then check splat spacing and total back width (19½"). Drill the pilot holes into E, apply glue, and drive the screws.

Note: *For joints that will stand up to the extremes of Mother Nature, use Titebond II water-resistant glue, slow-set epoxy, or resorcinol glue.*

3. Assemble the seat by standing both part G's on their bottom edge and parallel to one another 19½" (inside measurement) apart (countersunk holes to the outside). Now, place the rear beveled seat slat on top of both G parts, aligning it with the start-point marks. Drill the pilot holes. Then, apply glue to the ends on the underside of the slat, reposition it, and drive the two screws. Next, position the 15° beveled slat at the nose of the seat, and attach it the same way. Now, square the seat and attach the remaining seat slats, spacing them about ¼" apart.

4. Using a ⅜" plug cutter, cut 70 ⅜"-long plugs. Next, glue and insert the plugs in the counterbored holes in the seat slats and backrest. Let the glue dry, then sand the plugs flush.

5. Clamp the front legs (I) to part G using the dimensions on the Exploded View drawing (13½" to top of seat, and ¼" back from the front edge of the leg). Square each leg as shown *below*. Adjust, if necessary. Drill the pilot holes and drive the three screws in each leg.

6. Spread an even coat of glue on the mating half-lap joints on the two armrests (K) and the back

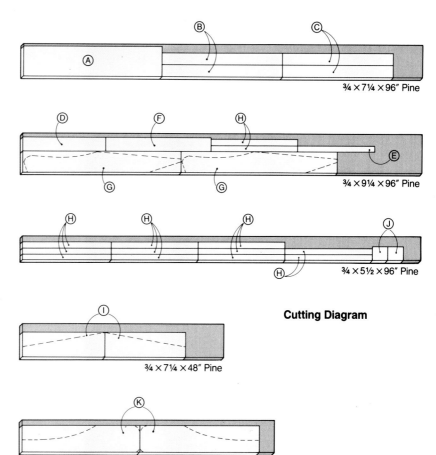

Cutting Diagram

support (F). Checking the inside corners for square, glue and clamp the pieces together.

7. Apply an even coat of glue to the top of the right front leg. Then, referring to the Armrest pattern, position the armrest assembly (F,K), lapping the armrests over the legs ¾" on the inside and ½" on the front edge. Holding the armrest steady (we used a couple of bar clamps), drill the pilot holes and drive the screws into each.

8. Next, attach the armrest supports (see the Exploded View drawing), driving the four screws into each.

9. Position and clamp the backrest assembly between the armrests and leg/seat supports, checking that the mating surface are flush. With the pieces correctly positioned, drill the pilot holes into both parts D and F, and drive the screws where shown on the drawing titled Attaching the Chair Back.

10. Glue and install the remaining plugs, let glue dry, and then sand the plugs flush.

11. Finish-sand the entire chair, and apply the exterior finish of your choice.

Project Tool List
Tablesaw
Bandsaw
Jointer
Disk sander
Portable drill
Drill press
   Bits: ⁷⁄₆₄", ⁵⁄₃₂", ⅜"
Belt sander
Finishing sander

Note: *We built the project using the tools listed. You may be able to substitute other tools or equipment for listed items you don't have. Additional common hand tools and clamps may be required to complete the project.*

continued

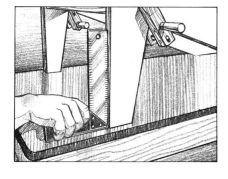

THE ADIRONDACK LAWN CHAIR

continued

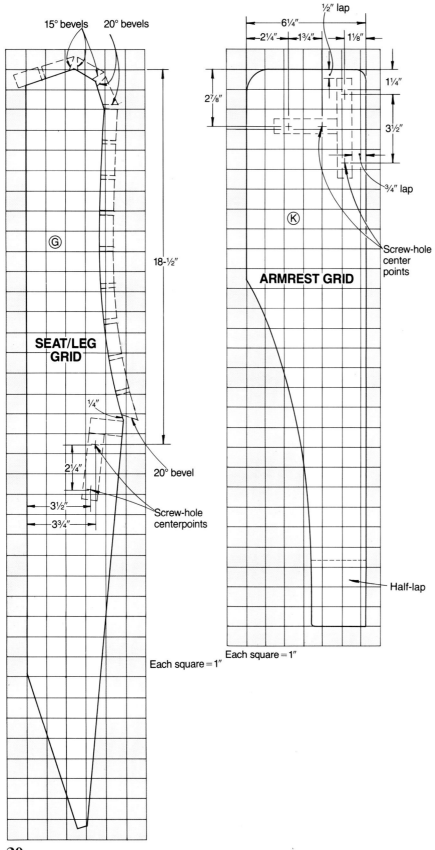

15° bevels   20° bevels

½" lap

6¼"

2¼"   1¾"   1⅛"

1¼"

2⅞"

3½"

¾" lap

ⓚ

Screw-hole
center
points

ARMREST GRID

18-½"

ⓖ

**SEAT/LEG
GRID**

¼"

20° bevel

2¼"

Screw-hole
centerpoints

3½"

3¾"

Half-lap

Each square = 1"

Each square = 1"

TWO-PART PATIO CHAIR

This stylish patio chair looks as great indoors as it does out. In fact, you may want to make more than one. The identically shaped pieces simplify construction, and also allow you to store the chair in a small closet space. Simply separate the parts, and slide the legs of the seat section between the back supports.

Note: Because of space limitations, we can't provide full-sized patterns for this project. However, to enable you to build the project, we've included gridded patterns. To enlarge these patterns, see the instructions on page 96.

Prepare the patterns, and then cut the parts

1. With a scissors, cut the full-sized back and seat supports (A,B) patterns to shape. Arrange the patterns on the face of one of the 1¹⁄₁₆ x9¼ x48" boards (we used white oak). See the Cutting Diagram on *page 24* for how we laid out the patterns. Next, apply spray adhesive to the undersides of both patterns and adhere them to the board. Apply double-faced tape to the underside of that board, and then stack it on top of a second 1¹⁄₁₆x9¼x48" board, aligning the boards along the edges.

2. Bandsaw the supports to shape as shown *right*. (We cut just outside the line, and then sanded to the line.) Separate the pieces, and remove the tape and patterns.

3. From ¾"-thick oak, rip and crosscut 25 seat and back slats (C), and the three crossbars (D, E, F) as dimensioned in the Bill of Materials. Rout a ¼" round-over along one edge of one seat slat. Finish-sand all parts.

4. Rip a ⁷⁄₁₆x⁷⁄₁₆x60" strip from scrap pine. From it, crosscut 28 spacers to 2" long for use later.

5. Chuck a combination ⅜" countersink/counterbore bit in your drill press. Next, clamp a fence to your drill press table, positioning it ½" from the centerpoint of the bit. Clamp a stopblock 2½" from the bit's centerpoint. Drill the holes in the back slats. (See the Screw Hole detail on *page 22* for hole and screw specifications.) Move the stopblock 3⅝" from the bit's centerpoint, and drill the seat slat holes.

6. With a ⅜"-diameter plug cutter, cut 56 plugs from ⁵⁄₁₆"-thick oak scrap (we planed thicker stock). You'll use the plugs later to fill the counterbored screw holes.

Next, assemble the chair

1. Cut two pieces of ¾"-thick plywood to 6x15⅞". Fit these

continued

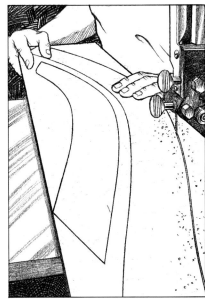

TWO-PART PATIO CHAIR

continued

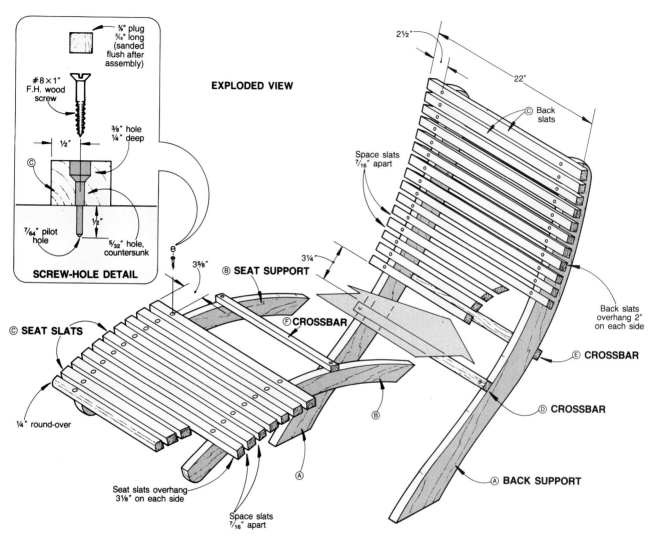

EXPLODED VIEW

⅜" plug
5/16" long
(sanded
flush after
assembly)

#8 × 1"
F.H. wood
screw

½"

⅜" hole
¼" deep

ⓒ

7/64" pilot
hole

½"

5/32" hole,
countersunk

SCREW-HOLE DETAIL

3⅝"

ⓔ

ⓒ **SEAT SLATS**

¼" round-over

Seat slats overhang
3⅛" on each side

Space slats
7/16" apart

ⓑ **SEAT SUPPORT**

3¼"

ⓕ **CROSSBAR**

ⓑ

ⓐ

2½"

22"

ⓒ Back
slats

Space slats
7/16" apart

Back slats
overhang 2"
on each side

ⓔ **CROSSBAR**

ⓓ **CROSSBAR**

ⓐ **BACK SUPPORT**

spacers between the back supports where shown at *right,* and then clamp.

2. Glue and screw one back slat at the top of the back supports (see the Side View drawing on *page 25*), aligning the edge flush with the ends of the supports. (We used Titebond II water-resistant glue; slow-set epoxy or resorcinol would also work.) Using a framing square, square the assembly as you work. Also, center the slat from side to side so it overhangs 1⅞" on both sides. (Once the slats were positioned, we drilled 7/64" pilot holes ½" deep into the supports,

ⓐ

¾ × 6 × 15⅞" spacers

ⓐ

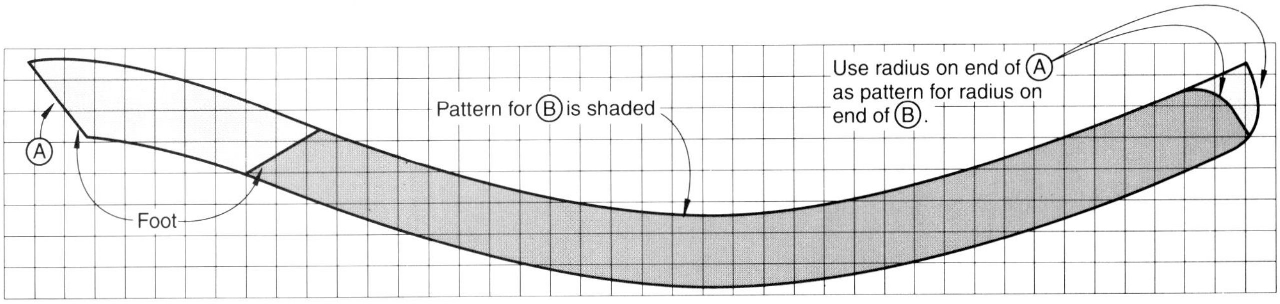
Pattern for (B) is shaded
Use radius on end of (A) as pattern for radius on end of (B).
(A)
Foot

SUPPORT PATTERNS

Each square=1"

Bill of Materials

Part	Finished Size* T	W	L	Mat.	Qty.
A* back sup.	1$\frac{1}{16}$"	8"	42"	O	2
B* seat sup.	1$\frac{1}{16}$"	6"	34"	O	2
C slats	¾"	1"	22"	O	25
D crossbar	¾"	1"	18"	O	1
E crossbar	¾"	1"	18"	O	1
F crossbar	¾"	1"	15¾"	O	1

* Parts marked with an * shown initial size. You cut them to final size during construction.

Material Key: WO–white oak.
Supplies: double-faced tape, 56–#8X1" flathead wood screws, scrap pine, ¾" plywood, water-resistant glue, finish of your choice.

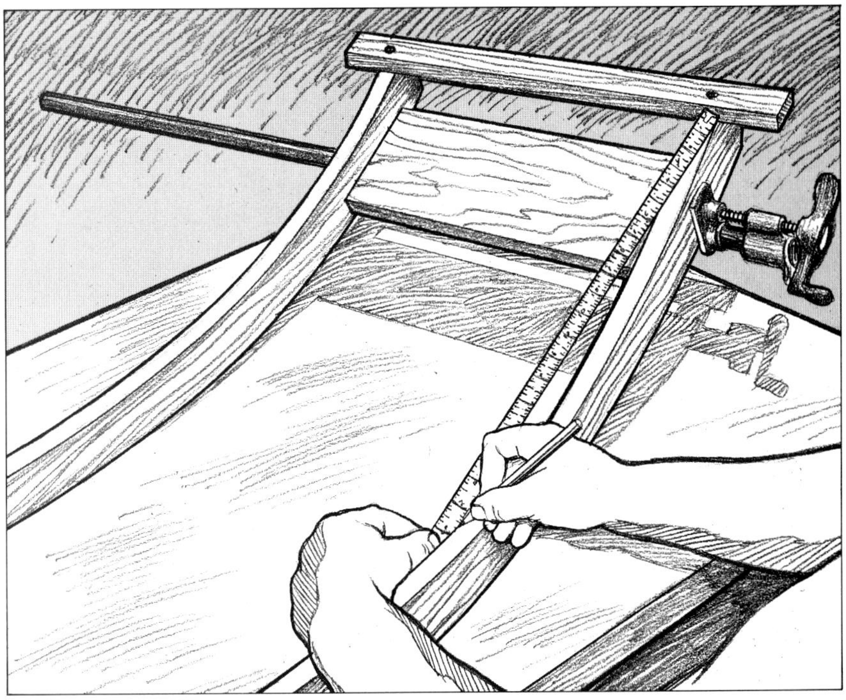

and waxed the screws before driving them.)

3. Butt the end of your tape measure against the inside edge of the top slat where shown at *right*. Now use a pencil to make a mark 20⅛" from that point on the edge of both back supports.

4. Lay, but don't fasten, 14 back slats on the back supports, spacing them with the $\frac{7}{16}$" spacer blocks cut earlier. The edge of the last slat should align with the marks you made in step 3. If it does not, resize the spacers so the last slat ends on those points. When you have spaced the slats correctly, glue and screw each slat to the back supports. Remove the spacers.

5. Measure 3¼" forward from the edge of the last slat along both back supports and mark. (See the Side View drawing.) Mark and then drill and counterbore the screw holes in the front crossbar (D). Attach this crossbar to the supports at this point.

6. To assemble the seat section, take the two plywood spacers you used for assembling the back supports and shorten both to 13⅝" long. Clamp them between the two seat supports (B) the same way you did when assembling the back section earlier.

7. Glue and screw the front slat with the rounded-over edge to the front of the seat supports. (See the Side View drawing on *page 25*.) When attaching the front slat, center it so 3⅛" overhangs on each side of the supports. Wipe off any glue squeeze-out. Square the assembly.

8. Measure 12$\frac{15}{16}$" from the back edge of the first slat, and mark both seat supports at that point. The edge of the last seat slat should butt against these marks.

9. Lay the rest of the seat slats across the seat supports, and space them with the $\frac{7}{16}$" spacer blocks. Adjust the spacing if necessary so the last slat ends on the marks. Now, glue and screw the slats to the seat supports. Remove all spacers.

10. Put the chair together in a sitting position where shown on the Exploded View drawing. Place the rear crossbar (E) against the back supports where shown on the

continued

TWO-PART PATIO CHAIR

continued

Side View drawing, and then clamp it as shown at *left*. Next, drill, glue, and then screw this crossbar in position permanently.

11. Attach the remaining crossbar (F) against the rear crossbar (E) where shown on the Side View drawing.

12. Glue the oak plugs in the holes in the slats, aligning the grain of the plugs with that of the slats. After the glue dries, sand the plugs flush with the surface of the slats. (We used a palm sander to speed the sanding.)

13. Test the fit of the seat section in the stored position inside the back section before finishing. (See the Stored Position drawing *opposite* for reference.) If the legs of the seat section do not slide easily in between the legs of the back section, sand the outside curved surfaces of the back supports until the seat slats clear.

14. Apply the finish. (Since we planned on using the chairs in a covered porch, we left the wood unstained and applied two coats of polyurethane. If you intend to leave your chair outdoors, consider using spar varnish or paint. We've also used Flood Clear Wood Finish, an oil-based wood preservative. This product applies easily, and can be reapplied as needed without much surface preparation.)

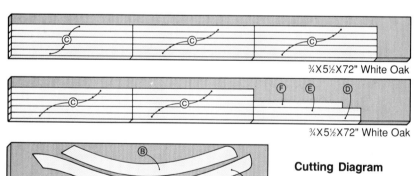

¾X5½X72" White Oak

¾X5½X72" White Oak

Cutting Diagram

1¹⁄₁₆X9¼X48" White Oak (2 pieces needed)

Project Tool List
Tablesaw
Bandsaw
Portable drill
Drill press
   Bits: $\frac{7}{64}$", $\frac{5}{32}$", $\frac{3}{8}$"
   $\frac{3}{8}$" plug cutter
Router
   $\frac{1}{4}$" round-over bit
Belt sander
Finishing sander

Note: *We built the project using the tools listed. You may be able to substitute other tools or equipment for listed items you don't have. Additional common hand tools and clamps may be required to complete the project.*

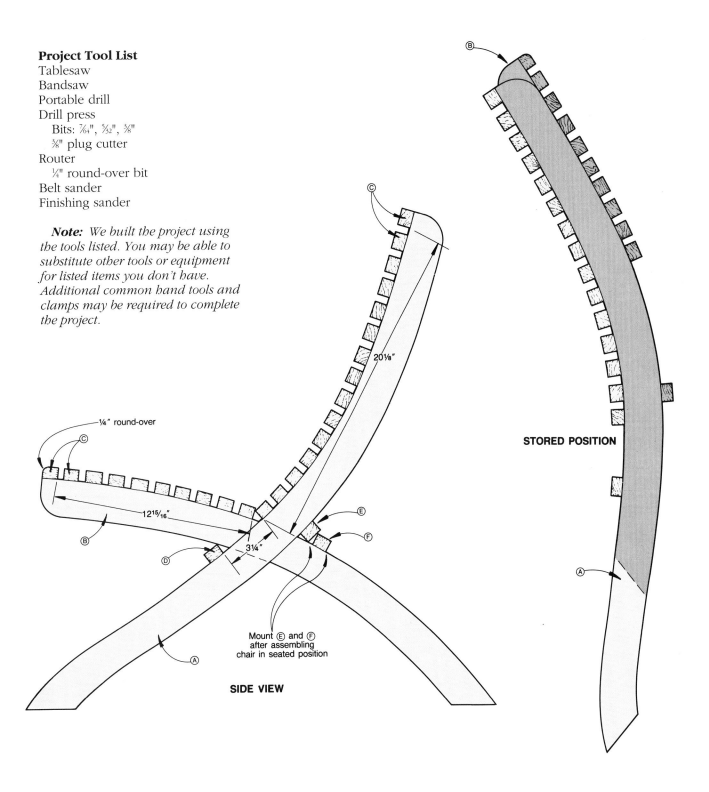

1/4" round-over

20⅛"

12¹⁵/₁₆"

3¼"

Mount Ⓔ and Ⓕ
after assembling
chair in seated position

SIDE VIEW

STORED POSITION

25

MAHOGANY OUTDOOR CHAIR

Tired of buying bargain-brand outdoor furniture and having it fall apart in a year or two? Are you ready for a table and chair set that will look as good in five years as it does today? Then, have we got a deal for you! Solidly built out of genuine (Honduras) mahogany and stylishly designed, this dynamic duo spells value.

Here we explain how to make the chairs; in the next project, we'll cover the table construction.

Note: Because of space limitations, we can't provide full-sized patterns for this project. However, to enable you to build the project, we've included gridded patterns. To enlarge these patterns, see the instructions on page 96.

Start with the legs

Note: You'll need some 2½"x2½" mahogany for the front and rear legs. We were able to purchase stock this size. If you have trouble locating stock this thick, laminate thinner stock to size. If you plan to use the table and chairs outdoors, use either slow-set epoxy, Titebond II water-resistant glue, or resorcinol glue.

1. Cut the two rear legs (A) and the two front legs (B) to the sizes listed in the Bill of Materials on *page 29.* Chamfer both ends of the rear legs and the bottom end of the front legs. (We chamfered ours on the tablesaw, with the blade set at 45° and the miter gauge fitted with an auxiliary fence to support the long stock.)

2. To form the curved sections (C) that attach to each front leg, cut a piece of 2½" square mahogany to 1³⁄₁₆"x2½"x12¾". Lay out the two curved sections (including the tenons) on the stock using the Front Leg grid on *page 31.*

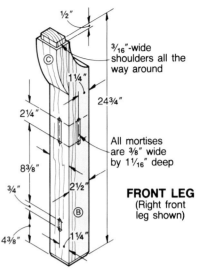

½″

³⁄₁₆″-wide
shoulders all the
way around

24¾″

1¼″

2¼″

All mortises
are ⅜″ wide
by 1¹⁄₁₆″ deep

8⅜″

¾″

2½″

FRONT LEG
(Right front
leg shown)

4⅜″

1¼″

3. Attach an auxiliary wooden fence to your tablesaw rip fence. Refer to the six-step drawing on *page 28* to form the top of each front leg.

Now, form the mortises in the legs

1. Mark the mortise centerpoints on the two rear legs (A) and the two front legs (B) where shown on the Rear and Front Leg drawings. Remember that you are working in pairs of A's and B's. When the legs are in the position shown on the Exploded View drawing, the corresponding mortises must face each other.

2. Form the mortises, following the four steps in the Mortise Forming detail accompanying the Rear Leg drawing on *page 28*.

Cut the tenons and the other frame members

1. Cut the top seat rails (D) and bottom rails (E) to the sizes listed in the Bill of Materials. Cut the stretcher (F) to size plus 1″ in length. Cut the support rails (G, H), seat slats (I, J), armrests (K), backrest bottom rail (L), and backrest top rail (M) to size. (Do not make the contour cuts on parts
continued

MAHOGANY OUTDOOR CHAIR

continued

REAR LEG
(Left rear leg shown)

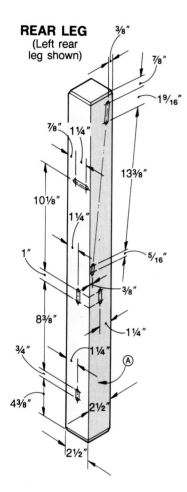

FORMING THE CURVED SECTION OF EACH FRONT LEG

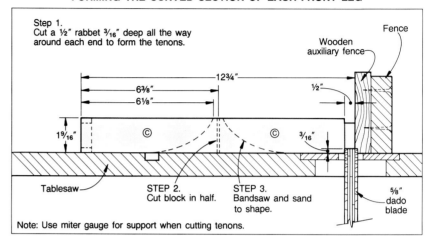

Step 1.
Cut a ½" rabbet ³⁄₁₆" deep all the way around each end to form the tenons.

Fence

Wooden auxiliary fence

Tablesaw

STEP 2.
Cut block in half.

STEP 3.
Bandsaw and sand to shape.

⁵⁄₈" dado blade

Note: Use miter gauge for support when cutting tenons.

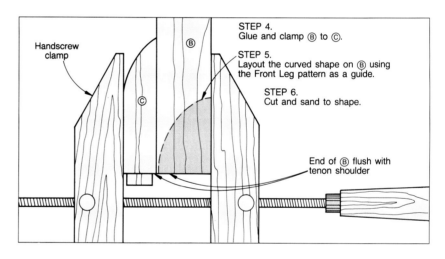

Handscrew clamp

STEP 4.
Glue and clamp ⒝ to ⒞.

STEP 5.
Layout the curved shape on ⒝ using the Front Leg pattern as a guide.

STEP 6.
Cut and sand to shape.

End of ⒝ flush with tenon shoulder

MORTISE FORMING DETAIL

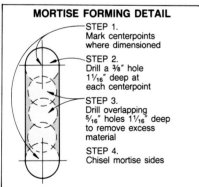

STEP 1.
Mark centerpoints where dimensioned

STEP 2.
Drill a ³⁄₈" hole 1¹⁄₁₆" deep at each centerpoint

STEP 3.
Drill overlapping ⁵⁄₁₆" holes 1¹⁄₁₆" deep to remove excess material

STEP 4.
Chisel mortise sides

D and K yet; you'll cut them to shape after tenoning.)

2. Cut tenons on both ends of the seat rails (D), bottom rails (E), and support rails (G, H), using the dimensions on the drawing titled Forming the Tenons. Refer to the Side Rail drawing for sizes, and cut the tenons on the side rails (D).

Then, referring to the Armrest drawing for the tenon size, cut the tenon on the back end of the armrests (K). Now, using the details on the Exploded View drawing for tenon sizes, cut a tenon on both ends of the backrest bottom and top rails (L, M).

3. Cut a ¾" dado ⅜" deep in each lower rail (E) where shown on the Exploded View drawing.

4. Cut the seat rails (D) to shape, using the Side Rail drawing as a guide.

5. Cut the armrests to final shape, using the Armrest drawing on *page 31* for reference.

6. Rout ⅜" round-overs along the top edges of the backrest top rail

(M). Then, mark and cut a ½" radius on each top corner of the backrest top rail (see the Backrest Top Rail detail accompanying the Exploded View drawing for reference). Sand each radius smooth with a 1" drum sander.

Assemble the end sections

1. Dry-clamp the legs (A, B/C) and rails (D, E). Square each assembly, and slide the tenon on the armrest (K) into its mating mortise in the rear leg. Hold the armrest firmly against the tenoned top of the front leg, and mark the location of the mortise needed on the *bottom* side of the armrest.

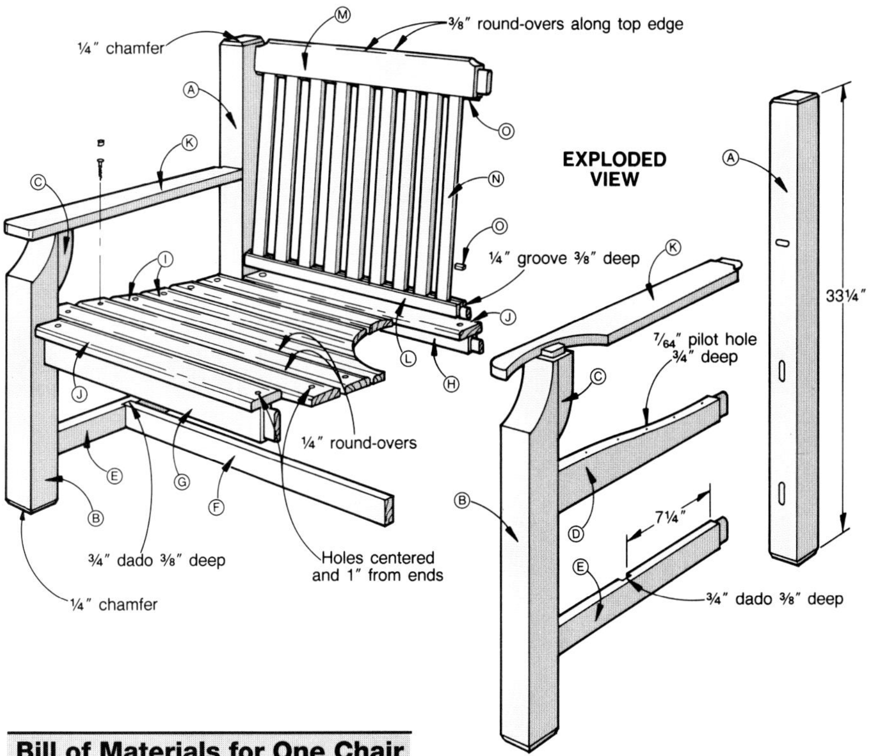

EXPLODED VIEW
¼" chamfer
⅜" round-overs along top edge
¼" groove ⅜" deep
⁷⁄₆₄" pilot hole ¾" deep
33¼"
¼" round-overs
7¼"
¾" dado ⅜" deep
Holes centered and 1" from ends
¾" dado ⅜" deep
¼" chamfer

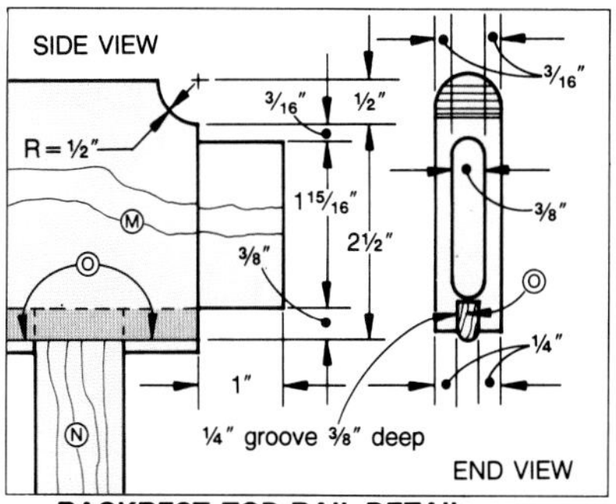

SIDE VIEW
R = ½"
³⁄₁₆"
½"
1¹⁵⁄₁₆"
2½"
⅜"
1"
¼" groove ⅜" deep
END VIEW
³⁄₁₆"
⅜"
¼"

BACKREST TOP RAIL DETAIL

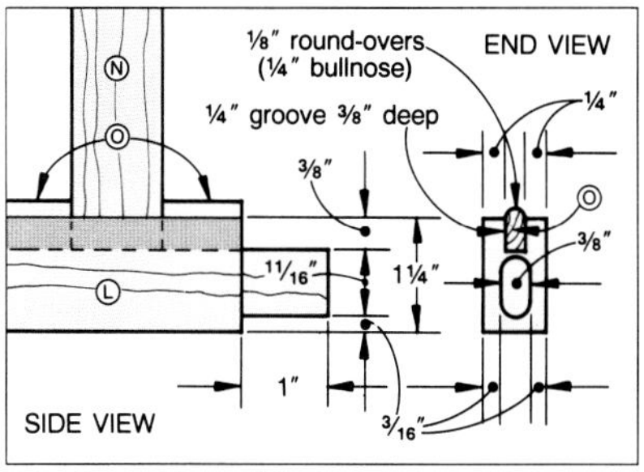

⅛" round-overs (¼" bullnose)
END VIEW
¼" groove ⅜" deep
⅜"
¹¹⁄₁₆"
1¼"
1"
SIDE VIEW
³⁄₁₆"
¼"
⅜"

BACKREST BOTTOM RAIL DETAIL

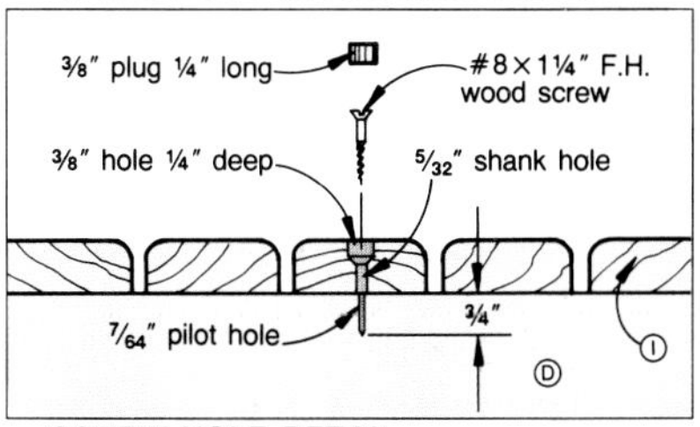

⅜" plug ¼" long
#8×1¼" F.H. wood screw
⅜" hole ¼" deep
⁵⁄₃₂" shank hole
⁷⁄₆₄" pilot hole
¾"

SCREW HOLE DETAIL

Bill of Materials for One Chair

Parts	Finished Size* T	W	L	Mat.	Qty.
A rear legs	2½"	2½"	33¼"	M	2
B front legs	2½"	2½"	24½"	M	2
C* curved sects	1 9/16"	2½"	6⅛"	M	2
D rails	¾"	3"	17¼"	M	2
E rails	¾"	1½"	17¼"	M	2
F* stretcher	¾"	1½"	21½"	M	1
G support rail	¾"	3"	21"	M	1
H support rail	¾"	1¾"	21"	M	1
I slats	¾"	2¼"	23½"	M	6
J front & back slat	¾"	2¼"	19"	M	2
K armrests	¾"	3¼"	18¾"	M	2
L backrest bot. rail	¾"	1¼"	21"	M	1
M backrest top rail	¾"	3"	21"	M	1
N splats	¼"	1 1/16"	13"	M	9
O* spacers	¼"	½"	15/16"	M	20

*Initially cut parts marked with an * oversized. Then, trim each to finished size according to the how-to instructions.

Material Key: M–mahogany

Supplies: water-resistant glue or slow-set epoxy, #8X1¼" F.H. wood brass screws, exterior finish.

Repeat with the other armrest. Remove the armrests, leaving the rest of the assembly dry-clamped.

2. To form the mortise on the *bottom* side of each armrest, use a ⅜" flat-bottomed bit (we used a Forstner), and drill a ½"-deep hole at each corner of your layout lines. Now, drill overlapping holes to remove stock, and chisel each mortise clean.

3. Check the fit of the armrests on the dry-clamped end sections. Again, remove the armrests; you'll add them later after you have attached the seat slats.

4. Glue and clamp each end section, checking for square. If you use epoxy, slip on vinyl gloves, and immediately wipe off excess epoxy with a clean cloth dampened with acetone. Acetone will remove uncured epoxy.

Complete the frame, and build the backrest

1. Dry-clamp the support rails (G, H) and backrest top and bottom (L, M) between the end assemblies. Check for square. Remove the clamps and disassemble.

2. Using the Backrest Top Rail detail on the Exploded View drawing as a guide, cut a ¼" groove ⅜" deep centered along the top edge of the backrest bottom rail (L) and along the bottom edge of the backrest top rail (M). (We cut the grooves on the tablesaw fitted with a ¼" dado blade. To keep the pieces firmly against the fence, we used a feather board.)

3. Rip five strips 1 1/16" wide by 13" long from ¾" mahogany stock. Now, resaw each strip to obtain two ¼X1 1/16X13" strips for the splats (N).

4. To form the spacers (O), start by cutting two strips ¼X½X24". Rout or sand an ⅛" round-over along one edge of each strip. To prevent the pieces from falling into the gaps in the insert around the saw blade, cover the area with masking tape. Next, clamp a

continued

MAHOGANY OUTDOOR CHAIR
continued

To safely cut the short spacers, use the eraser end of a pencil to clear the spacers from the blade.

Brush glue into the groove in the backrest lower rail, and then add the spacers and splats.

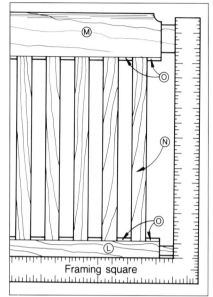

Framing square

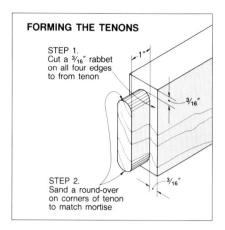

FORMING THE TENONS

STEP 1.
Cut a ³⁄₁₆" rabbet on all four edges to from tenon

1"

³⁄₁₆"

STEP 2.
Sand a round-over on corners of tenon to match mortise

³⁄₁₆"

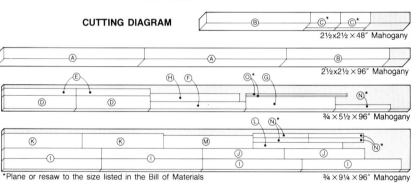

CUTTING DIAGRAM

2½x2½ × 48" Mahogany

2½x2½ × 96" Mahogany

¾ × 5½ × 96" Mahogany

*Plane or resaw to the size listed in the Bill of Materials

¾ × 9¼ × 96" Mahogany

scrap block to the fence about 2" in front of the blade. Raise the saw blade ⅜" above the saw table. Position the fence so the block is ¹⁵⁄₁₆" from the inside edge of the blade. Using your miter-gauge fence for support, slide one end of one of the strips against the block. Push the piece over the blade to cut a spacer, and carefully move the spacer away from the blade with the eraser end of a pencil as shown in the photo *above, top.*

5. Starting at one end with a spacer, glue the spacers and splats into the ¼" groove in the bottom rail as shown in the second photo *above.* Wipe off the excess glue.

6. Once you have all the spacers and splats in position in the bottom rail, apply glue in the groove in the top rail. Lay the bottom-rail splat assembly flat on a work surface, and add the top rail to the ends of the splats. Glue the spacers in place. With a framing square, check that the splats are square to the rails and that the ends of the tenons are aligned.

Assemble the chair and add the finish

1. Glue and clamp the support rails (G, H) and the backrest assembly between the end sections, checking for square. Next, measure the distance between the dadoes in

the lower rails (E), and cut the stretcher (F) to fit. Glue the stretcher in place.

2. Using the Screw Hole detail accompanying the Exploded View drawing for reference, drill plug and shank holes through the seat slats (I, J).

3. Rout a ¼" round-over along the top edges (not ends) of each seat slat. Clamp the front slat (J) to the chair, centering the predrilled screw holes over the front support rail (G). Drill pilot holes into the seat rails (D), and screw the front slat in place.

4. Cut two strips of scrapwood to ¼" thick for use as spacers.

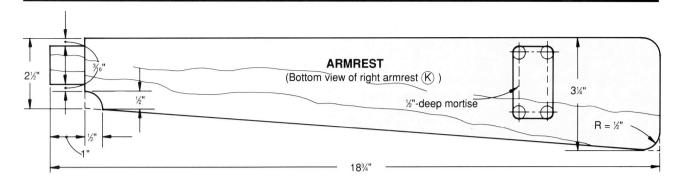

ARMREST
(Bottom view of right armrest Ⓚ)

½"-deep mortise

R = ½"

2½"

³⁄₁₆"

½"

½"

1"

3¼"

18¾"

Working towards the back, space the slats (I) ¼" apart with the scrap spacers, and screw the slats to the top seat rails (D). Locate the rear slat (J) and screw it in place.

5. Plane a piece of mahogany to a ⁵⁄₁₆" thickness and cut sixteen ⅜"-diameter plugs from it. With the grain direction on the plugs going in the same direction as the slats, plug the screw holes and sand the plugs flush.

6. Glue and clamp the armrests (K) in position.

7. Sand the entire chair smooth. Stain and finish as desired. (For the first coat, we sprayed on spar varnish—reduced 25 percent with mineral spirits. After this dried, we lightly sanded with 320-grit sandpaper, and then applied two additional coats full strength.) To prolong the life of the finish, store the pieces indoors (under cover) over the winter months. Also, if you happen to dent or scratch the finish, touch up the blemish with spar varnish to prevent moisture from getting under the finish.

Project Tool List
Tablesaw
    Dado blade or dado set
Bandsaw
Portable drill
Drill press
    Bits: ⁷⁄₆₄", ⁵⁄₃₂", ⁵⁄₁₆", ⅜"
    ⅜" plug cutter
Drum sander, 1"
Router
    ⅛" round-over, ¼" round-over, ⅜" round-over
Belt sander
Finishing sander

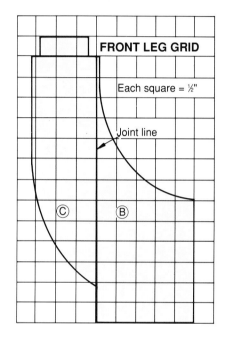

FRONT LEG GRID

Each square = ½"

Joint line

Ⓒ   Ⓑ

Note: *We built the project using the tools listed. You may be able to substitute other tools or equipment for listed items you don't have. Additional common hand tools and clamps may be required to complete the project.*

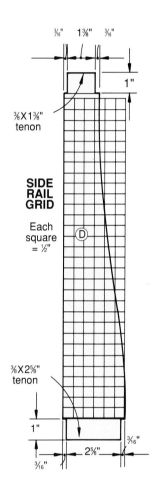

³⁄₁₆"   1⅜"   ³⁄₁₆"

1"

⅜ X 1⅜" tenon

SIDE RAIL GRID

Each square = ½"

Ⓓ

⅜ X 2⅝" tenon

1"

2⅝"

³⁄₁₆"

³⁄₁₆"

MAHOGANY OUTDOOR TABLE

For a durable outdoor table to match those gorgeous mahogany chairs, we designed this 48"-square table. It features mortise-and-tenon joinery and a top with splined miter joints. Once completed, this handsome project will give you years of enjoyable service.

Note: If you plan to use the table outdoors, use either slow-set epoxy, *Titebond II water-resistant glue, or resorcinol glue.*

Start with the legs

1. Laminate thinner stock face-to-face to form the 3¾6"-square legs. (We cut three pieces of 1¹⁄₁₆" thick stock to 3⅜" wide by 29" long. Then, we glued and clamped the pieces with the edges and ends flush. Later, after the glue dried, we scraped off the excess glue from one edge,

planed that edge smooth, and then ripped the opposite edge for a 3¾6" finished width. Finally, we crosscut the legs to length.)

2. Following the four steps on the Mortise detail accompanying the Exploded View drawing, form the mortises on two adjoining faces of each of the four legs.

3. Cut or rout ¼" chamfers along the bottom end of each leg.
continued

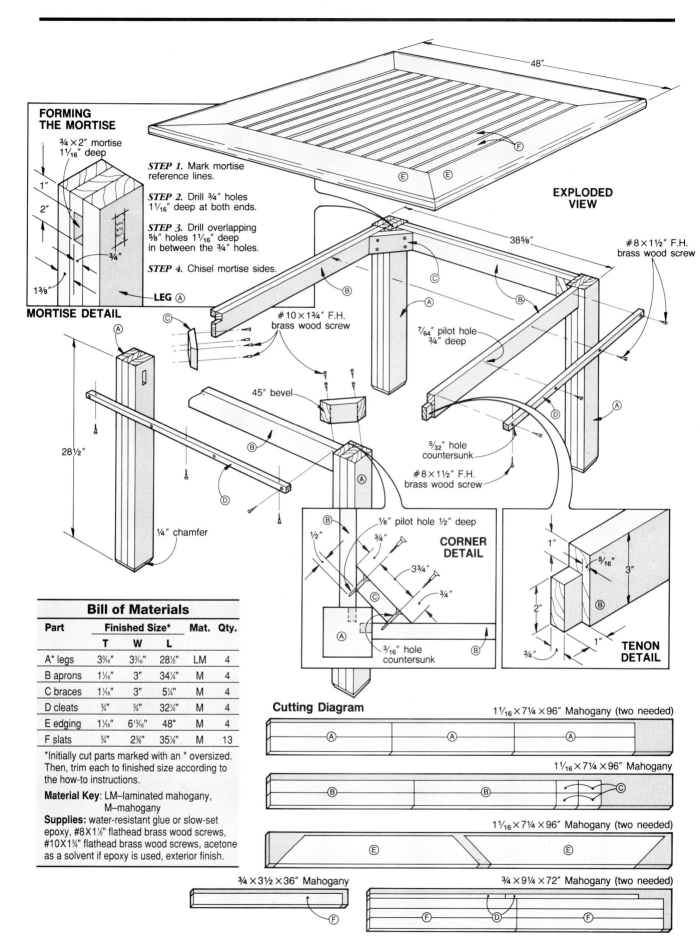

FORMING THE MORTISE

¾ × 2″ mortise 1¹⁄₁₆″ deep

1″
2″
1³⁄₈″
¾″

STEP 1. Mark mortise reference lines.

STEP 2. Drill ¾″ holes 1¹⁄₁₆″ deep at both ends.

STEP 3. Drill overlapping ⅝″ holes 1¹⁄₁₆″ deep in between the ¾″ holes.

STEP 4. Chisel mortise sides.

LEG Ⓐ

MORTISE DETAIL

48″

EXPLODED VIEW

38⅝″

#8 × 1½″ F.H. brass wood screw

#10 × 1¾″ F.H. brass wood screw

⁷⁄₆₄″ pilot hole ¾″ deep

45° bevel

28½″

¼″ chamfer

⁵⁄₃₂″ hole countersunk

#8 × 1½″ F.H. brass wood screw

⅛″ pilot hole ½″ deep

½″
¾″

CORNER DETAIL

3¾″
¾″
¾″

³⁄₁₆″ hole countersunk

1″
3″
⁵⁄₁₆″
2″
1″
¾″

TENON DETAIL

Bill of Materials

Part	Finished Size*			Mat.	Qty.
	T	W	L		
A* legs	3³⁄₁₆″	3³⁄₁₆″	28½″	LM	4
B aprons	1¹⁄₁₆″	3″	34¼″	M	4
C braces	1¹⁄₁₆″	3″	5¼″	M	4
D cleats	¾″	¾″	32¼″	M	4
E edging	1¹⁄₁₆″	6¹³⁄₁₆″	48″	M	4
F slats	¾″	2⅜″	35⅛″	M	13

*Initially cut parts marked with an * oversized. Then, trim each to finished size according to the how-to instructions.

Material Key: LM–laminated mahogany, M–mahogany

Supplies: water-resistant glue or slow-set epoxy, #8X1½″ flathead brass wood screws, #10X1¾″ flathead brass wood screws, acetone as a solvent if epoxy is used, exterior finish.

Cutting Diagram

1¹⁄₁₆ × 7¼ × 96″ Mahogany (two needed)

Ⓐ Ⓐ Ⓐ

1¹⁄₁₆ × 7¼ × 96″ Mahogany

Ⓑ Ⓑ Ⓒ

1¹⁄₁₆ × 7¼ × 96″ Mahogany (two needed)

Ⓔ Ⓔ

¾ × 3½ × 36″ Mahogany

Ⓕ

¾ × 9¼ × 72″ Mahogany (two needed)

Ⓕ Ⓓ Ⓕ

MAHOGANY OUTDOOR TABLE

continued

Add the tenoned aprons

1. Rip and crosscut the four aprons (B) to size (1⅟₁₆×3×34¼").

2. Cut the tenons to size on each end of each apron—see the Tenon detail for reference. (To cut the tenons, we mounted a dado blade to our tablesaw and attached a long auxiliary fence to our miter gauge to support the legs when cutting the tenons.)

3. Dry-fit the tenons in the mortises to check the fit. Spread slow-set epoxy or water-resistant glue on the mating surfaces and clamp one apron between two legs. With a framing square, check that the legs are square to the apron. If you use epoxy, slip on vinyl gloves, and immediately wipe off excess epoxy with a clean cloth dampened with acetone. Acetone will remove uncured epoxy. Repeat with another apron.

Glue or epoxy two aprons between the two leg/apron assemblies to complete the base. Again, check that the legs are square to the aprons.

4. Cut the four corner braces (C) to size, mitering the ends at 45°. Viewing the Corner detail accompanying the Exploded View drawing for reference, drill and countersink four mounting holes in each corner brace.

5. Cut a V-shaped notch in one face of four 4"-long pieces of 2×4. As shown in the drawing *above right,* glue and clamp each corner brace in place.

6. Using the previously drilled shank holes in the braces as guides, drill ⅛" pilot holes ½" into the aprons where shown on the Corner detail on *page 33.* Drive #10×1¾" screws through the braces and into the aprons to further strengthen the joint.

7. Cut the cleats (D) to size. Drill and countersink four mounting holes in each cleat. With the top edges flush, screw them to the aprons (B).

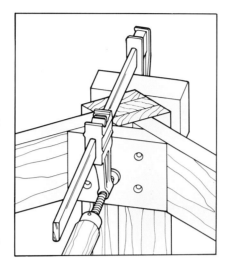

Now, let's build and assemble the tabletop

1. Cut the edging pieces (E) to size, mitering the ends at 45°.

2. Cut or rout a ⅜" groove ⅜" deep ⅜" from the top surface along the inside edge of *two* pieces of the edging. See the Slat detail for reference before making the cut.

3. Fit your router with a ¼" slotting cutter. Viewing the Spline and Slot details accompanying the Tabletop drawing *below* and the photo *opposite* for reference, rout a pair of ¼" slots ½" deep in each mitered end of each edging piece.

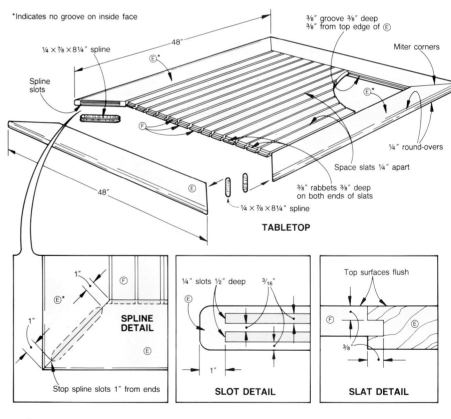

*Indicates no groove on inside face

¼ × ⅞ × 8¼" spline

Spline slots

48"

⅜" groove ⅜" deep ⅜" from top edge of Ⓔ

Miter corners

¼" round-overs

Space slats ¼" apart

⅜" rabbets ⅜" deep on both ends of slats

¼ × ⅞ × 8¼" spline

48"

TABLETOP

SPLINE DETAIL

1"

1"

Stop spline slots 1" from ends

SLOT DETAIL

¼" slots ½" deep

³⁄₁₆"

1"

SLAT DETAIL

Top surfaces flush

⅜"

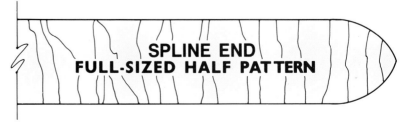

SPLINE END FULL-SIZED HALF PATTERN

Rout a pair of slots and cut a pair of spliner for each mitered corner joint.

4. From ¼" stock (we resawed thicker stock), cut eight pieces to ⅞×8¼" for the splines. Before cutting, note the direction orientation in the photo. If the grain runs the length of the spline, the spline will have a tendency to split when the edging expands. Now, cut or sand the ends of each spline to the shape shown on the full-sized Spline pattern. Set the splines aside for now.

5. Cut 13 slats (F) to the size listed in the Bill of Materials.

6. Cut or rout a ⅜" rabbet ⅜" deep across both ends of each slat.

7. Dry-clamp the tabletop parts (including the splines) to check the fit. Trim if necessary.

8. Brush glue or epoxy on all mating surfaces and splines, and clamp the tabletop assembly (E, F, and splines), checking for square. Wipe off excess epoxy with an acetone-dampened cloth. (To space

the slats ¼" apart, we used pieces of ¼" dowel stock as spacers.)

9. Sand the top of the tabletop smooth and flush.

10. Rout ¼" round-overs along the top and bottom outside edges of the tabletop.

Sand and finish

1. Finish-sand the base and tabletop. Stain and finish. (We left the wood natural. For the first coat of finish, we sprayed on spar varnish—reduced with mineral spirits 25 percent. Later, we lightly sanded with 320-grit sandpaper, and then applied a second and later a third coat full strength.)

To prolong the life of the finish, store the table and chairs indoors over the winter months. Also, if you happen to dent or scratch the finish, touch-up the blemish with spar varnish to prevent moisture from getting under the finish.

2. Set the tabletop upside down on a blanket. Secure the tabletop to the base with #8×1½" flathead brass wood screws threaded through the cleats (D).

Project Tool List
Tablesaw
   Dado blade or dado cutter
Portable drill
Drill press
   Bits: ⅞₄", ⅛", ⁵⁄₃₂", ³⁄₁₆", ⅝", ¾"
Router
   ¼" round-over, ¼" slotting cutter
Belt sander
Finishing sander

Note: *We built the project using the tools listed. You may be able to substitute other tools or equipment for listed items you don't have. Additional common hand tools and clamps may be required to complete the project.*

FOLDING SNACK TABLE

When company comes, whether your event takes place indoors or out, having an extra surface to set things on can be a big help. That's why we developed this stylish oak folding table. For those who made the two-part chair on *page 21*, you'll find this table a perfect companion for it.

Note: Because of space limitations, we can't provide full-sized patterns of the Folding Snack Table shown here. For your convenience, we'll supply you with full-sized patterns for the leg. See page 96 for details. Or, if you just can't wait to get started, enlarge the gridded pattern shown opposite.

Begin making the legs

1. Draw a 1"-square grid on a 4X27" sheet of paper. Following the Gridded Leg Pattern *opposite,* draw the leg pattern on the gridded paper. (Or, start with the full-sized pattern.) Now, cut around the pattern with scissors.

2. Rip and crosscut four pieces of ¾"-thick oak to 4X27". (See the Cutting Diagram *opposite.*) Apply double-faced tape to the top surface of two pieces and stack the remaining pieces on these. Apply spray

adhesive to the back of the pattern and adhere it to the top of one stack. Saw out the two legs simultaneously. (We used a bandsaw and cut just outside the line.)

3. Sand the legs to the line while they are taped together. (We used a drum sander for the inside curve; a disc sander for the outside curve and the rounded ends.)

4. Place the leg set on the remaining stack and pencil around it to transfer the shape. Cut out and sand the second set of legs.

5. Chuck a ⅛" bit into your drill press. Now, stack the legs with the pattern onto the other set, align, and then drill holes through the top set and into the bottom where indicated by the pattern. Separate the two sets. Next, drill ¾" holes through the top end and middle of one set where marked by the small holes. (We backed the legs with scrap to prevent chip-out.) Drill a ¾" hole through the top end only of the other set. (See the Exploded View drawing *opposite.*)

6. Switch to a ¹³⁄₁₆" bit and drill through the center of the second leg set (inside pair) where marked. Remove the pattern, separate the legs, remove the tape, and finish-sand.

Make the tabletop

1. Rip and crosscut two oak pieces to dimensions listed in the Bill of Materials for the tabletop supports (B). Using the Tabletop End detail on the Exploded View, mark the centerpoints for the ¹³⁄₁₆" holes at each end of the supports. Drill the holes.

2. Using a compass, scribe the ⅞" radius at each end. Bandsaw and sand the ends. Mark and bandsaw the notch in each support.

3. From ¾" oak, rip and cross-cut 15 pieces to the dimensions listed in the Bill of Materials for table slats (C). (You'll use one of these as a spacer later.) Sand the pieces.

4. Using a ⅜" countersink/ counterbore bit, drill holes 1⅜" in

from the ends and centered on the top face. (We set up a fence and stop block to drill holes at the same location.)

5. Saw a piece of ¾" plywood scrap to 11½X20" for use as a spacer. Place the table supports (B) on their bottom edge and parallel to one another on a flat surface. Insert the plywood spacer between the supports and square the supports with a square. Clamp with bar clamps.

6. Center and align the first slat flush at one end of the supports. Next, drill a ⁷⁄₆₄" hole through the countersunk/counterbored hole at one end of the slat and ¾" into the support. Screw one slat to the support as shown *below.* Attach the slat at the opposite end.

7. Place the ½"-wide spacer cut in step 3 on edge against the inside edge of the first slat and position the second slat alongside it. Center, drill, and screw it in place. Install the remaining slats. Place the last slat flush with the supports at the opposite end.

Plywood spacer

Assemble the table

1. From a ¾" dowel, cut two 13⅛" lengths and one 11½" length. Cut four 1¼" lengths from a ¼" dowel.

2. Cut a V-block from a 2X4 scrap measuring 12" long. Using the Exploded View drawing for reference, mark the centerpoints for the ¼" holes on the 13⅛"-long dowel at the unnotched end of the table, and on the center leg hinge dowel.

Bill of Materials

Part	Finished Size*			Mat.	Qty.
	T	W	L		
A* legs	¾"	4"	27"	O	4
B tabletop sup.	¾"	2"	20½"	O	2
C** slats	½"	1"	15"	O	15

* Parts cut to final size during construction.
** Included is one extra slat used as a spacer.

Material Key: O–oak
Supplies: 28–#8X1" flat head wood screws,
2d finish nails, 2–¾"-diameter oak dowels,
1–¼"-diameter oak dowel.

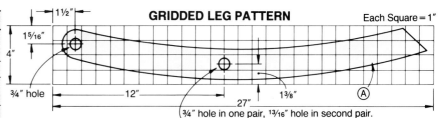

GRIDDED LEG PATTERN   Each Square = 1"

¾" hole in one pair, ¹³⁄₁₆" hole in second pair.

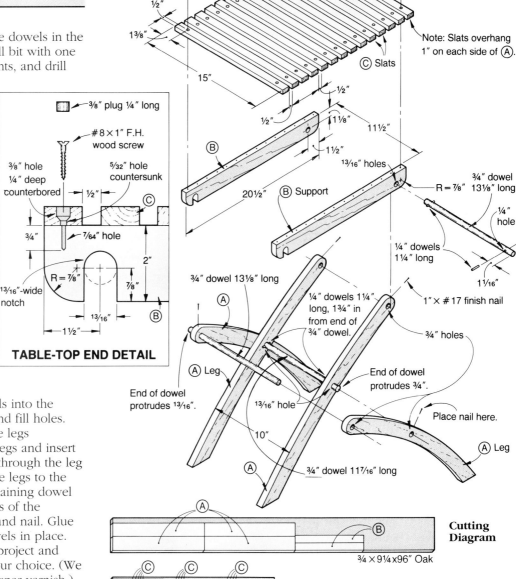

Next, place one of the dowels in the V-block, align the drill bit with one of the hole centerpoints, and drill the hole. Drill the other hole. Finally, drill the holes in the remaining dowel the same way.

3. Lay the tabletop upside down. Place the drilled ends of the inside legs along the inside of the unnotched ends of supports B. Slip the 13⅛"-long dowel through the supports and leg end holes. Center the dowel. Next, drill pilot holes through the ends of the legs for 2d finish nails. Drive nails into the holes, set the nails, and fill holes.

4. Place the outside legs alongside the inside legs and insert the 11½"-long dowel through the leg holes. Nail the outside legs to the dowel. Insert the remaining dowel through the end holes of the outside legs, center, and nail. Glue and insert the ¼" dowels in place.

5. Finish-sand the project and apply the finish of your choice. (We applied two coats of spar varnish.)

TABLE-TOP END DETAIL

Project Tool List

Tablesaw
Bandsaw
Portable drill
Drill press
  Bits: ¹⁄₁₆", ⁷⁄₆₄", ⁵⁄₃₂", ¼", ⅜", ¾", ¹³⁄₁₆"

Drum sander
⅜" plug cutter
Disk sander
Belt sander
Finishing sander

Cutting Diagram

¾ × 9¼ x96" Oak

¾ × 5½ × 48" Oak

Note: *We built the project using the tools listed. You may be able to substitute other tools or equipment for listed items you don't have. Additional common hand tools and clamps may be required to complete the project.*

FOR OUR FINE-FEATHERED FRIENDS

With any one of the bird feeders or birdhouses described on the following pages, you can invite a flock of fine-feathered creatures into your garden and provide them with a treat.

BARN BIRDHOUSE

We engineered our handsome barn birdhouse to include small openings along the bowed roof for ventilation, and drain holes inside to prevent moisture from collecting. We also screwed the base to the sides, allowing you to unscrew it to clean out the birdhouse come next spring.

First, frame the barn

1. Cut the barn front and back (A), and the sides (B), to the sizes listed in the Bill of Materials from ¾"-thick exterior plywood. (See the Exploded View drawing *below* for reference.) From the same stock, cut the base (C) to size.

Note: *We used exterior-grade plywood instead of solid wood because of its ability to endure the weather, and because it doesn't bow as solid wood does when kerfed.*

2. With double-faced tape, tape the front and back pieces together face to face. Using carbon paper, transfer the full-sized pattern on *page 41* to the top piece. Mark the centerpoint for the 1¼" entrance hole. Bandsaw or scrollsaw the end pieces to shape as shown *above right*. Sand the cut edges

with a disk sander, and separate the pieces. Remove the tape.

3. Now, drill the 1¼" entrance hole in the barn front. (We used a spade bit mounted in a drill press.)

4. With the edges and ends flush and the good sides of the plywood facing out, glue and nail the barn sides between the front and back pieces. (We used resorcinol, a waterproof glue suited for outdoors.)

Next, cut the kerfs

1. Raise your tablesaw blade ¹⁄₁₆" above the surface of the saw table. Find the exact center of the front piece, and align it with the saw blade. Lock the saw's fence against
continued

continued

EXPLODED VIEW

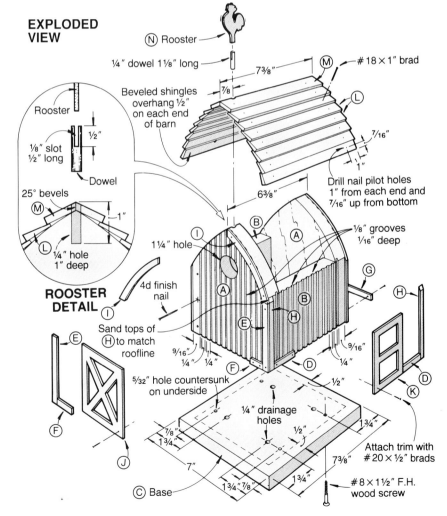

ROOSTER DETAIL

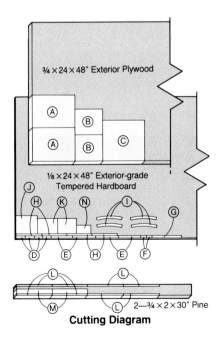

Cutting Diagram

BARN BIRDHOUSE
continued

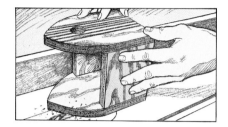

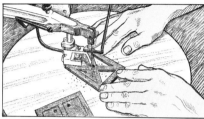

the front piece. Cut a kerf along the centers of the barn front and back pieces as shown *above*. Move the fence ⅜" further away from the blade, and cut a kerf on each side of the first kerf on both pieces. (See the full-sized pattern for kerf locations.) Reposition the fence ⅜" farther and cut another pair of kerfs in each piece. Continue the process to cut 13 kerfs in both pieces.

2. Repeat the procedure in step 1 to cut the decorative kerfs in both side pieces. Note that the last side kerfs actually are cut into the edges of the front and back pieces.

3. Prime the outside (leave the inside unfinished) of the barn assembly and base with an exterior primer. Next, paint the outside of the barn sides with exterior red; the base with exterior green.

Cut and add the trim

1. Rip two ⅜"-wide strips from a 24×48" piece of ⅛" exterior-grade tempered hardboard. From these, crosscut trim pieces D, E, F, and G, using the dimensions on the Bill of Materials. Rip a ¼"-wide strip from the same piece of hardboard and crosscut the trim pieces labeled H.

2. Using carbon paper, transfer the full-sized patterns (*opposite*) of the four curved trim pieces (I), the front door (J), the two side doors (K), and the rooster (N) onto the remaining hardboard. Cut the pieces to shape using a bandsaw or scrollsaw. (We made the inside cuts by drilling starter holes, and then sawing as shown *top right.*)

3. Prime and paint the trim and door pieces white.

4. After the paint dries, glue and nail on the trim and doors where shown on the Exploded View drawing. (To drive the nails into the hardboard trim, we clipped the head off a 4d finish nail. Then, we chucked the nail in a hand drill and used it to drill the pilot holes.)

Raise the roof!

1. For the beveled shingles, first cut two pieces of ¾×2×30" pine and square the edges on both. Tilt your tablesaw blade 10° from vertical. Position the saw fence ³⁄₃₂" away from the bottom of the blade as shown in the detail *below*. Next, carefully bevel-rip each edge on the two pieces to make four beveled strips. Now, crosscut 14 pieces (L) to 7⅜" long from the strips.

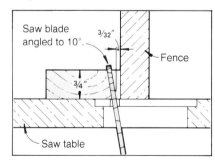

Saw blade angled to 10°. ³⁄₃₂"
Fence
¾"
Saw table

2. To make the two top roof boards (M), first square the edges on one of the remaining pine pieces you bevel-cut in step 1 *above*. Next, set the saw's fence ¼" from the side of the blade. Turn the piece on edge and resaw a ¼"-thick strip from it. Now, tilt the saw blade 25° from center. Adjust the saw fence so you bevel-rip the strip to ⅞" final width. Finally,

crosscut two 7⅜"-long roof pieces from the strip.

3. Prime, and later paint the roof boards brown. Next, using the full-sized pattern as a positioning guide, glue and nail (we used 1" brads and drilled pilot holes to avoid splitting) the shingles to the barn assembly. (Laying the assembly's front, and then back, on the pattern, we first marked the start location for the shingles on the bowed edges as shown *below*. Then, we attached the shingles beginning with the bottom course.) Set the nails, fill the holes, and retouch with the roof paint.

continued

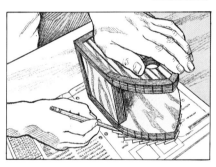

Bill of Materials

Part	Initial Size*			Mat.	Qty.
	T	**W**	**L**		
A	¾"	5¾"	7¾"	ex. plywood	2
B	¾"	4⅜"	4⅝"	ex. plywood	2
C	¾"	7"	7⅜"	ex. plywood	1
D	⅛"	⅜"	1½"	t. hardbrd	4
E	⅛"	⅜"	4⅛"	t. hardbrd	4
F	⅛"	⅜"	1⅛"	t. hardbrd	2
G	⅛"	⅜"	5⁵⁄₁₆"	t. hardbrd	1
H	⅛"	¼"	4⁷⁄₁₆"	t. hardbrd	4
I	⅛"	¾"	4¾"	t. hardbrd	4
J	⅛"	3"	3¹³⁄₁₆"	t. hardbrd	1
K	⅛"	2⅝"	3⅜"	t. hardbrd	1
L	⁷⁄₃₂"	¾"	7⅜"	pine	14
M	¼"	⅞"	7⅜"	pine	2
N	⅛"	1⅜"	2½"	t. hardbrd	1

Supplies: double-faced tape, carbon paper, 4d finish nails, #18X1" brads, #20X½" brads, 1¼" pipe 7½'-long threaded at one end, 1¼" pipe flange, 4–#10X½" flathead wood screws, 4–#8X1½" flathead wood screws, ¼" dowel.

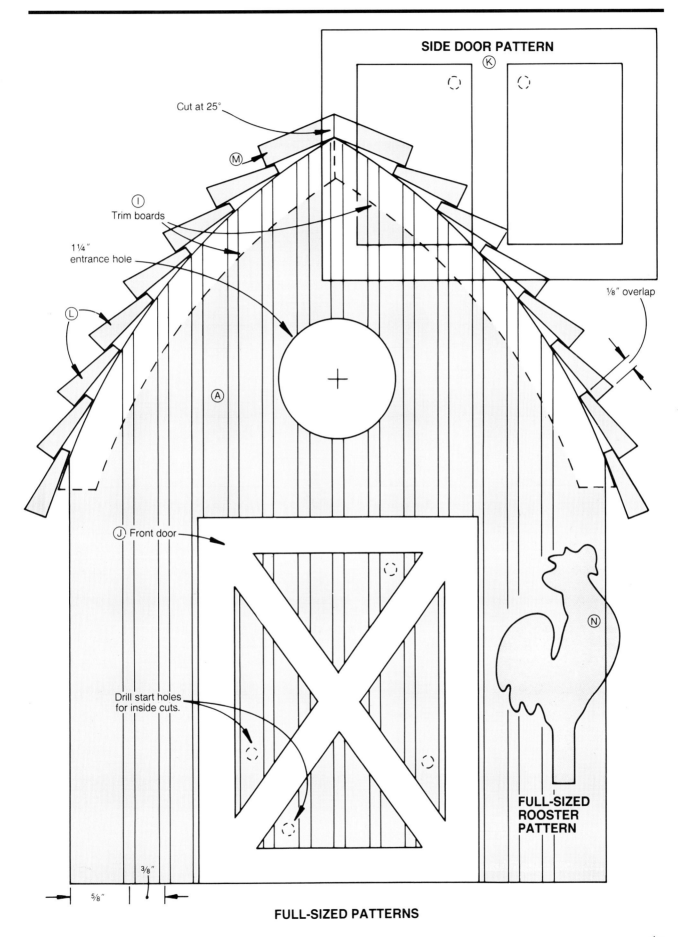

SIDE DOOR PATTERN

K

Cut at 25°

M

I
Trim boards

1¼″
entrance hole

L

⅛″ overlap

A

J Front door

Drill start holes
for inside cuts.

N

**FULL-SIZED
ROOSTER
PATTERN**

³/₈″

⁵/₈″

FULL-SIZED PATTERNS

BARN BIRDHOUSE
continued

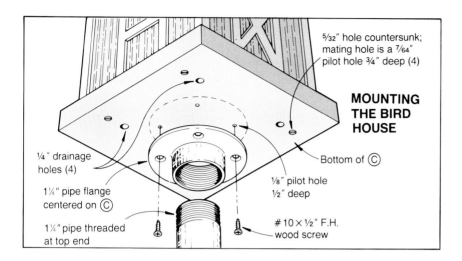

5/32" hole countersunk; mating hole is a 7/64" pilot hole 3/4" deep (4)

MOUNTING THE BIRD HOUSE

1/4" drainage holes (4)

1 1/4" pipe flange centered on C

1 1/4" pipe threaded at top end

Bottom of C

1/8" pilot hole 1/2" deep

#10 × 1/2" F.H. wood screw

Add the rooster and pipe flange

1. Cut a 1/4" diameter dowel to 1 1/8" length. Cut a 1/8"-wide slot 1/2" deep in one end. Glue the rooster—cut earlier—in the slot. Prime the rooster and dowel; later, paint it red.

2. Drill a 1/4" hole 1" deep through the center roof boards and into the barn front where shown on the Exploded View drawing. Glue the rooster-dowel assembly in the hole.

3. Referring to the Exploded View drawing and the Mounting the Birdhouse drawing *above,* drill four 1/4" drain holes through the base. Next, drill and countersink the four screw holes for attaching the barn to the base. Finally, screw, but do not glue, the barn to the base.

4. Center, drill the pilot holes, and then screw a 1 1/4" threaded pipe flange to the underside of the base. Sink a 1 1/4" pipe that's threaded at the top end into a posthole in the ground so that 5' of the pipe extend above the ground and another 2 1/2' extend below. Plumb the pipe, and then set it in

concrete. After the concrete cures, screw on the birdhouse and keep an eye out for your first feathery occupants.

Project Tool List

Tablesaw
Bandsaw or scrollsaw
Portable drill
Drill press
   Bits: 7/64", 1/8", 5/32", 1/4", 1 1/4"
Disk sander
Finishing sander

Note: *We built the project using the tools listed. You may be able to substitute other tools or equipment for listed items you don't have. Additional common hand tools and clamps may be required to complete the project.*

FINE-FEATHERED FRIEND FEEDER

We were astounded while scouting garden stores for bird feeders. As you've probably noticed, run-of-the-mill bird feeders, built from ½" cedar and stapled together, run short on design and practicality. Yuck!

We think you—and your feathered friends—will like this hexagonal feeder. It holds a whopping 10 pounds of seed and features a large 15"-diameter feeding tray.

Start with the hexagonal column

Note: We used ¾" cedar for our bird feeder; redwood also would work. If you select ¾" cedar, it will have one rough side. You can either plane or belt-sand the rough side smooth. For joints that will stand

up to the extremes of Mother Nature, use Titebond II water-resistant glue, slow-set epoxy, or resorcinol glue.

1. Rip and crosscut six pieces of ¾"-thick cedar to 4½" wide by 18½"

long for the column sections (A).

2. Tilt your tablesaw blade 30° from vertical. Bevel-rip *one* edge of each column section. Reposition the fence, and bevel-rip the opposite edge of each for 4"-wide pieces. (We cut scrap stock first to check for accurate 30° cuts.)

3. Lay out a notch on the bottom end of each piece. See the Notch Detail accompanying the Exploded View drawing for reference. Cut the notches to shape (we cut ours on the bandsaw).

4. As shown in Step 1 of the two-step drawing *below,* position the column sections with the beveled edges facing down. Butt the pieces together with the notched ends flush. Using masking tape, join the six pieces. In addition to holding the pieces together, the tape prevents the adhesive from squeezing out onto the column exterior. Flip over the assembly and apply adhesive to the mating edges. (We used a small brush to completely coat both surfaces of each joint with glue.)

5. As shown in Step 2 of the drawing, roll the column assembly together, tape the remaining joint, and secure the column with band clamps. Then, remove the band clamps and tape. Sand the column smooth.

continued

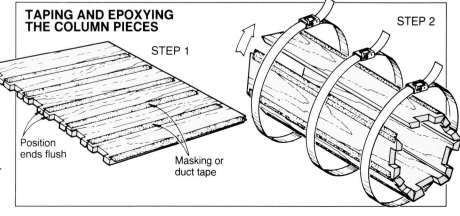

TAPING AND EPOXYING THE COLUMN PIECES

STEP 1

Position ends flush

Masking or duct tape

STEP 2

FINE-FEATHERED FRIEND FEEDER

continued

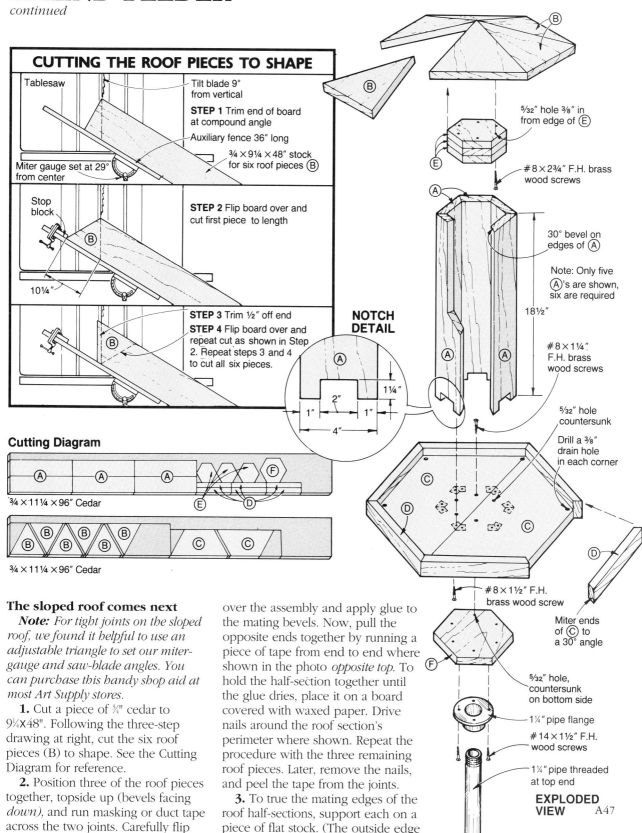

CUTTING THE ROOF PIECES TO SHAPE

Tablesaw

Tilt blade 9° from vertical

STEP 1 Trim end of board at compound angle

Auxiliary fence 36" long

¾ × 9¼ × 48" stock for six roof pieces (B)

Miter gauge set at 29° from center

Stop block

STEP 2 Flip board over and cut first piece to length

10¼"

STEP 3 Trim ½" off end

STEP 4 Flip board over and repeat cut as shown in Step 2. Repeat steps 3 and 4 to cut all six pieces.

NOTCH DETAIL

1¼"
2"
1" 1"
4"

Cutting Diagram

(A)   (A)   (A)   (F)

(E)   (D)

¾ × 11¼ × 96" Cedar

(B) (B) (B) (C) (C)
(B) (B) (B)

¾ × 11¼ × 96" Cedar

5/32" hole ⅜" in from edge of (E)

#8 × 2¾" F.H. brass wood screws

30° bevel on edges of (A)

Note: Only five (A)'s are shown, six are required

18½"

#8 × 1¼" F.H. brass wood screws

5/32" hole countersunk

Drill a ⅜" drain hole in each corner

#8 × 1½" F.H. brass wood screw

Miter ends of (C) to a 30° angle

5/32" hole, countersunk on bottom side

1¼" pipe flange

#14 × 1½" F.H. wood screws

1¼" pipe threaded at top end

EXPLODED VIEW   A47

The sloped roof comes next

Note: *For tight joints on the sloped roof, we found it helpful to use an adjustable triangle to set our miter-gauge and saw-blade angles. You can purchase this handy shop aid at most Art Supply stores.*

1. Cut a piece of ¾" cedar to 9¼×48". Following the three-step drawing at right, cut the six roof pieces (B) to shape. See the Cutting Diagram for reference.

2. Position three of the roof pieces together, topside up (bevels facing *down),* and run masking or duct tape across the two joints. Carefully flip

over the assembly and apply glue to the mating bevels. Now, pull the opposite ends together by running a piece of tape from end to end where shown in the photo *opposite top.* To hold the half-section together until the glue dries, place it on a board covered with waxed paper. Drive nails around the roof section's perimeter where shown. Repeat the procedure with the three remaining roof pieces. Later, remove the nails, and peel the tape from the joints.

3. To true the mating edges of the roof half-sections, support each on a piece of flat stock. (The outside edge

Bill of Materials

Part	Finished Size*			Matl.	Qty.
	T	W	L		
A* column pieces	¾"	4"	18½"	C	6
B* roof pieces	¾"	9¼"	10¼"	C	6
C* seed-tray pieces	¾"	7½"	17¼"	EC	2
D banding	¾"	1½"	9½"	C	6
E roof supports	¾"	5⅜"	6¼"	C	3
F seed-tray support	¾"	7"	8"	C	1

* Initially cut parts marked with an * oversized. Then, trim each to finished size according to the how-to instructions.

Material Key: C–cedar, EC–edge-joined cedar
Supplies: waxed paper, masking tape, #8X1¼" flathead brass wood screws, #8X1½" flathead brass wood screws, #8X2¾" flathead brass wood screws, #14X1½" flathead wood screws, 1¼" pipe flange, 1¼" pipe threaded on one end, exterior finish.

Trim the mating edge of each roof half-section on the tablesaw.

of the middle section must be flush with the outside edge of the flat stock.) As shown *above*, trim about ⅛" off the mating edge of each roof half-section.

4. Apply glue to the mating edges, and tape together the two roof sections. Later, sand the roof.

Next, build the seed tray

1. To form the tray (C), start by cutting two pieces of ¾" cedar to 7½x 17¼" long, miter-cutting the ends at a 30° angle where shown on the Seed Tray Drawing.

2. Glue the two pieces together edge to edge. After the glue dries, sand the tray surfaces.

3. Cut the banding pieces (D) to length, miter-cutting the ends at 30°. Check the fit against the tray, then

Drive nails into a scrap board around the perimeter of the roof half-section to hold the assembly together until the glue dries.

SEED TRAY

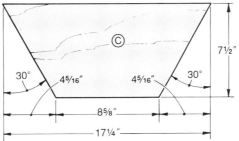

ROOF SUPPORT

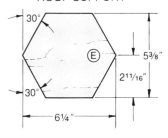

SEED-TRAY SUPPORT

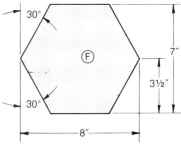

glue and clamp (or tape) the banding strips to the tray.

Cut the remaining pieces and assemble the feeder

1. Center the hexagonal column on the seed tray. Trace around the edges where the bottom end of the column comes in contact with the tray. Remove the column and drill a pair of 5/32" holes inside each outline (see the Exploded View drawing for reference). Viewing the same drawing for reference, drill a ⅜" drain hole in each corner of the tray. Screw (no adhesive) the column to the tray.

2. Cut the roof supports (E) and seed-tray support (F) to shape, using the drawings *above* for reference. With the edges and ends flush, glue together the three roof supports. Check the fit of the roof support inside the column. Trim or sand the edges of the roof support if necessary for a good fit.

3. Center the roof-support lamination (E) on the bottom side of the roof (B). Drill holes, and then glue and screw the roof support to the bottom of the roof. Repeat procedure to center and fasten the seed-tray support (F) to the bottom side of the tray (C).

4. Stain and finish. (We left ours unstained, and sealed the wood with two coats of Thompson's Water Seal.) Center and screw a 1¼" pipe flange to the bottom of the tray support. Bury the bottom end of a 1¼" pipe 30" in the ground, and mount the feeder.

Project Tool List
Tablesaw
Bandsaw
Drill press
  Bits: 5/32", ⅜"
Finishing sander

Note: *We built the project using the tools listed. You may be able to substitute other tools or equipment for listed items you don't have. Additional common hand tools and clamps may be required to complete the project.*

A TREAT FOR TWEETS
BIRD FEEDER

It takes only a little heart and a little heart redwood to show the local bird population you care. Add to this our heart-shape feeder design and you'll be only an evening away from creating a stir in your backyard. We covered our feeder with a metal flashing roof, to protect the food area, and hung it from a chain.

Make the heart-shape ends

1. Crosscut two pieces of 1×10 redwood to 10" lengths, or edge-join narrow stock to make like panels.

2. With carbon paper, make a full heart pattern on a sheet of paper using the Full-Size (Half) Heart Pattern *opposite.* Transfer all marks.

3. Place double-faced tape on the face of one panel. Stick this panel to the second, aligning the edges. Trace the heart and nail locations on top panel.

4. Using a band saw or scroll saw, cut the heart-shape ends (A). Saw outside the line, then sand to it. These form the heart-shape ends shown on the Exploded View drawing *below.*

5. Chuck a ⅜" piloted round-over bit into your table-mounted router. Roundover the outside edge of one heart, then turn the hearts over and rout the second one's outside edge.

6. Drill the five nail pilot holes through both hearts. (We backed them with scrap to prevent chip-out.)

7. Separate the hearts. Position the heart pattern on the *inside* face of one end and transfer the lines locating the roof support and tray. Mark the inside face of the other heart.

Make the tray and roof

1. Plane or resaw a 20" length of 1×6 redwood to ½" thickness. To form the tray (B), rip the piece to 5" wide and crosscut it to 8" long.

2. Plane or resaw the remaining ½×5" stock to ¼" thickness. Rip two 1¼"-wide strips and crosscut both to 8" long for the tray sides (C).

3. Rip and crosscut two pieces of ¾" redwood to 1¼×7¼". Place double-faced tape on the face of one piece, then stick both together, aligning the edges. Trace the Full-Size Roof Support Pattern (D) *opposite* onto one piece. Cut the part to shape. Separate the pieces, then mark and cut a ¼"-wide ⅜"-deep dado in both.

4. To form the roof edge (E), rip a piece of ¾" redwood to 1⅛" wide and crosscut it to 7¼" long. Test-assemble the roof parts making sure the assembly measures 8" long. Epoxy the joints and clamp the roof assembly until the glue hardens.

5. Using tin shears and wearing protective gloves, cut a strip of aluminum flashing to 8×9¾". To form the bent ends on the roofing, make a metal-bending jig. (We ripped a 1"

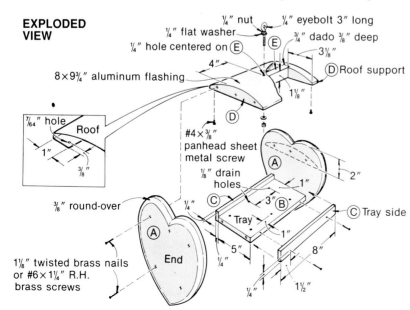

EXPLODED VIEW

deep saw kerf ⅛" in from the edge on a 12" length of 1×3" pine.) Slide one end of the flashing into the cut slot, place it on a flat surface, and slowly fold the pine back to bend the aluminum as shown *above*. Now, bend the other end of the flashing.

6. Slide the shaped-aluminum onto the roof frame, making it flush at both ends. Mark the four screw locations with an awl (see the Roof Detail on the Exploded View drawing), drill pilot holes, and drive the screws.

7. Using a rule, locate the center point of the roof and mark it with an awl. (If you plan to attach the feeder to a post or building, skip this step.) Drill a ¼" hole through the aluminum and the roof ridge. Assemble the eyebolt.

Now, assemble the feeder

1. Drill the two holes in the tray sides and the six drain holes in the tray.

2. Apply epoxy to the two long edges of the tray and nail the tray sides to them. Stand the feed tray upright and place a heart-shape end, routed side up, on top of it. Position the heart so the tray aligns with the tray location lines. Drill through the pilot holes (in the heart) and ½" into the tray. Remove the heart, apply epoxy to the end of the tray, reposition the tray again, and tap in the two brass nails. (We found the twisted brass nails at a well-stocked hardware store. You may substitute #6×1¼" roundhead brass screws for the nails.)

3. Position the roof assembly and align with the roof lines. Drill through the predrilled holes and ½" into the roof support. Apply epoxy to the roof support end. Now, reinstall the roof, align, and tap in the three nails.

4. Turn the partially assembled feeder end-for-end. Position the remaining heart-shape end on top of

the feeder and attach it to the roof and tray as outlined in steps 2 and 3. Set it aside and let the epoxy cure.

5. Finish if you desire. (We left the redwood parts unfinished so it will weather naturally.)

Project Tool List
Tablesaw
Bandsaw or scrollsaw
Router
   Router table
   Bits: ⅜" round-over, ¾" straight
Portable drill
   Bits: ⁷⁄₆₄", ⅛", ¼"
Finishing sander

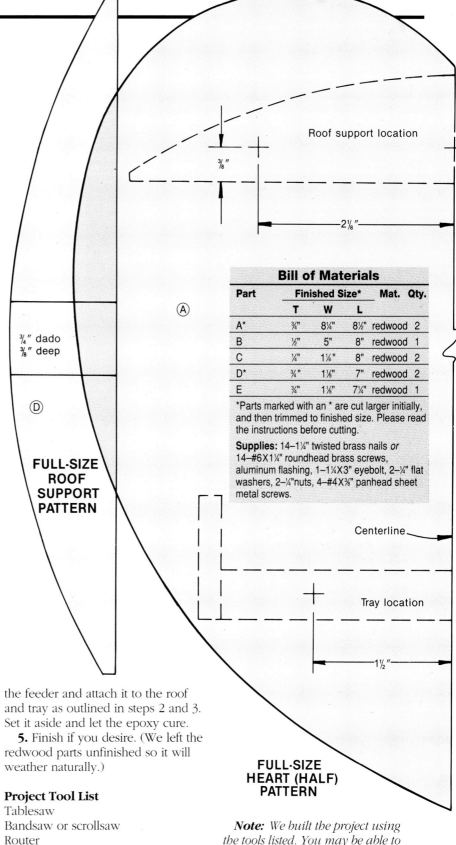

Roof support location

¾"

2⅛"

Ⓐ

FULL-SIZE ROOF SUPPORT PATTERN

¾" dado
⅜" deep

Ⓓ

Bill of Materials					
Part	**Finished Size***			**Mat.**	**Qty.**
	T	**W**	**L**		
A*	¾"	8¼"	8½"	redwood	2
B	½"	5"	8"	redwood	1
C	¼"	1¼"	8"	redwood	2
D*	¾"	1⅛"	7"	redwood	2
E	¾"	1⅛"	7¼"	redwood	1

*Parts marked with an * are cut larger initially, and then trimmed to finished size. Please read the instructions before cutting.

Supplies: 14–1¼" twisted brass nails *or* 14–#6X1¼" roundhead brass screws, aluminum flashing, 1–1¼X3" eyebolt, 2–¼" flat washers, 2–¼"nuts, 4–#4X⅜" panhead sheet metal screws.

Centerline

Tray location

1½"

FULL-SIZE HEART (HALF) PATTERN

Note: *We built the project using the tools listed. You may be able to substitute other tools or equipment for listed items you don't have. Additional common hand tools and clamps may be required to complete the project.*

FARMERS' SEED COMPANY BIRD FEEDER

Birds love to congregate around real-life country elevators in their search for sustenance. So they'll feel right at home when they discover this pint-sized feeder in your own backyard.

Note: For joints that will stand up to the extremes of Mother Nature, use Titebond II water-resistant glue, slow-set epoxy, or resorcinol glue.

Let's start building

1. Cut the sides (A), back (B), and front (C) from ½" exterior plywood to the size plus 1" in length.

2. Mark kerf locations 1" center-to-center on the face of the plywood pieces *opposite* the good face, noting their location on the Exploded View drawing. Using a tablesaw, cut deep kerfs in the good face of each plywood piece.

3. Lay out the roof pitch on the top end of each side piece, using the dimensions on the Exploded View drawing. Cut the rooflines where marked. Next, cut a 30° bevel on the *top end* of the front and back. Cut the sides, back, and front to finished length.

4. Cut the bottom (D) and the feed slide (E) to size, bevel-ripping both *edges* of the slide at 45°

5. Glue and nail the back (B) to the bottom (D), checking for square. Glue and nail the sides (A) to the back and bottom assembly. Then, glue the feed slide inside the assembly (we used masking tape to hold the slide in place).

6. Spread glue on the side edges of the front (C), spread the sides (A) apart slightly, slide the front in position, and nail it in place. The front's bottom should stop ¾" above the bottom (D) for the feed to pass through.

Building the roof and the feeding shed

1. To make the removable gable roof and shed roof, cut three roof parts (F) to size, bevel-ripping one side edge of each at 30°. Lay out and cut the roof supports (G) to shape, using the drawing *below* as a guide.

2. Spread glue on the beveled edges of the gable roof sections, and tape them together as shown in the drawing *right*. Remove the tape after the glue has dried. Then, glue and tape the supports in position where dimensioned on the Exploded View drawing.

3. Cut a strip of plywood 1¼" wide by 16" long for the feeder sides (H) and front (I). Mark the kerf locations 1" center-to-center, and cut the kerfs in the long strip. (For safety reasons we cut these kerfs on our radial arm saw by raising the blade ⅜" above the

surface of the table.) Cut the sides and front to finished lengths so the kerfs are located where shown on the Exploded View drawing.

4. Glue and nail the sides and front to the feeder assembly.

5. Cut the front pillars (J) to size, miter-cutting the top end of each at 30°. Spread glue on the mating surfaces of parts H and I, and clamp the pillars in position.

6. Spread glue on the top of the pillars and on the beveled edge of the lower roof (F). Tape the roof in position so it overlaps the feeder ½" on each side. Remove the tape after the glue has dried.

Finishing up

1. Sand smooth, and paint the birdfeeder as desired. (To get the weathered look, we applied exterior latex paint to one side at a time, waited about 30 seconds, and then wiped off just enough paint to expose the wood grain.) After the paint dries, fill the kerfs between the shed roof and front piece (C) with clear silicone to keep water from running down the elevator front and into the seed tray.

2. Use the half-sized pattern on the *opposite page* as a guide to make the decorative sign. (We cut a

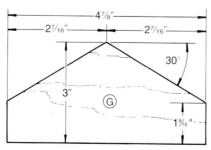

GABLE ROOF SUPPORT

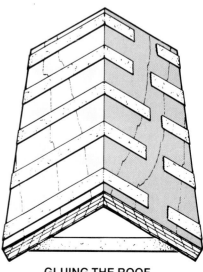

GLUING THE ROOF

Bill of Materials

Part	Finished Size* T	W	L	Mat.	Qty.
A*	½"	6"	17¾"	ext. plyw.	2
B*	½"	8"	16¼"	ext. plyw.	1
C*	½"	8"	15"	ext. plyw.	1
D	½"	8"	8"	ext. plyw.	1
E	½"	5"	8"	ext. plyw.	1
F	½"	4½"	10"	ext. plyw.	3
G	½"	3"	4⅞"	ext. plyw.	2
H	½"	1¼"	2½"	ext. plyw.	2
I	½"	1¼"	9"	ext. plyw.	1
J	¾"	¾"	5½"	pine	2

*Parts marked with an * are cut larger initially, and then trimmed to finished size. Please read the instructions before cutting.

Supplies: glue, 4d galvanized nails, gray exterior latex paint, clear silicone sealant, 1–1¼" pipe, 1–1¼" flange with #10X⅝" flathead sheet-metal screws, ⅛" acrylic, 2–#4X½" roundhead wood screws, masking tape, enamel paints for sign

piece of ⅛" clear acrylic to the shape of the sign and drilled two 7/64" mounting holes through the acrylic. Then, we lightly sanded the front of the acrylic with 320-grit sandpaper and painted the sign with an enamel paint on the sanded surface. Finally, we screwed the sign to the front of the elevator.)

3. Center and mount a 1¼" pipe flange to the bottom of the feeder. Mount the feeder to a 1¼" pipe that has the top end threaded to mate with the flange. Lift the gable roof assembly off the elevator, fill with bird feed, and watch the birds come home to roost.

EXPLODED VIEW

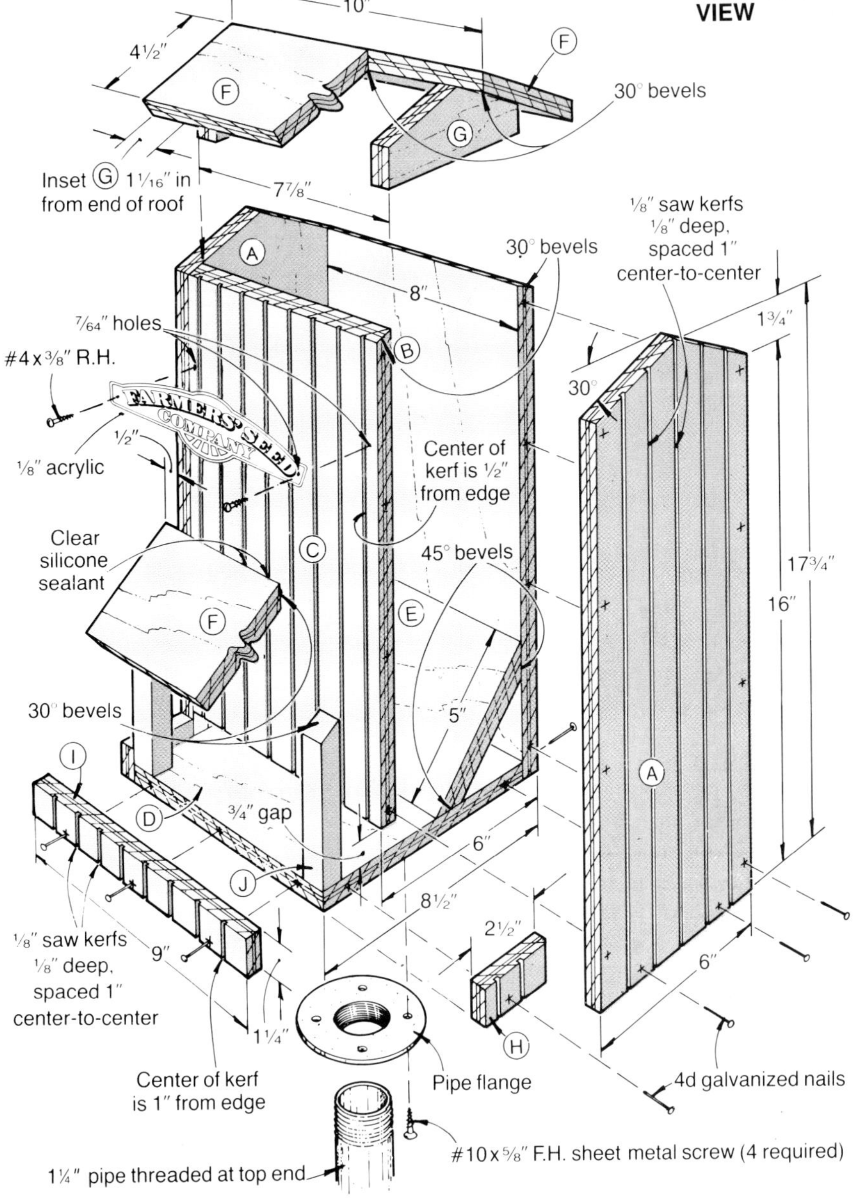

10"
4½"
F
30° bevels
G
Inset G 1 1/16" in from end of roof
7⅞"
⅛" saw kerfs ⅛" deep, spaced 1" center-to-center
A
30° bevels
8"
7/64" holes
#4 x ⅜" R.H.
B
1¾"
30°
½"
⅛" acrylic
Center of kerf is ½" from edge
Clear silicone sealant
C
45° bevels
17¾"
16"
E
F
30° bevels
5"
I
A
D
¾" gap
6"
J
8½"
2½"
⅛" saw kerfs ⅛" deep, spaced 1" center-to-center
9"
6"
1¼"
H
Center of kerf is 1" from edge
Pipe flange
4d galvanized nails
#10 x ⅝" F.H. sheet metal screw (4 required)
1¼" pipe threaded at top end

Project Tool List

Tablesaw
Radial-arm saw
Portable drill
  Bits: 7/64"
Finishing sander

Note: *We built the project using the tools listed. You may be able to substitute other tools or equipment for listed items you don't have. Additional common hand tools and clamps may be required to complete the project.*

Cutting Diagram

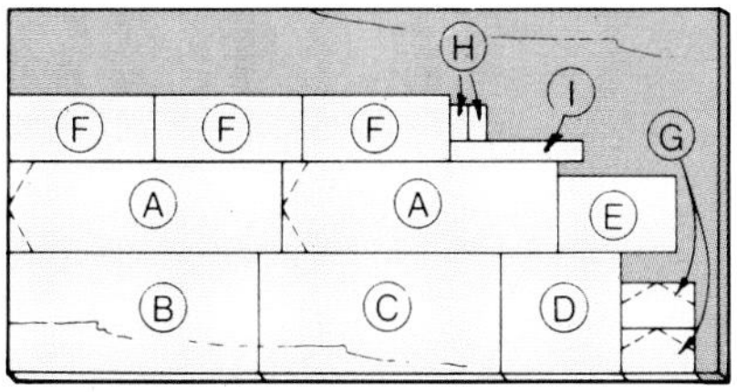

H
I
F
F
F
G
A
A
E
B
C
D

½ x 24 x 48" Exterior Plywood

HALF-SIZED PATTERN

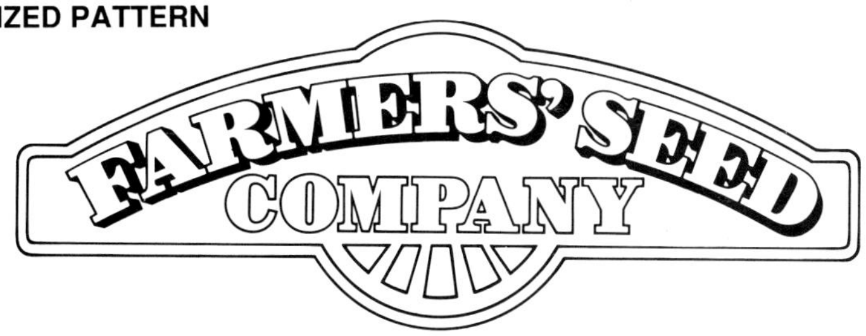

FARMERS' SEED
COMPANY

FLIGHT SCHOOL BIRDHOUSE

Here's a birdhouse design that always draws repeat visitors. And when it's time to clean out the house for a new family, you'll certainly enjoy the convenience of its easy-to-remove floor.

Note: The United States Department of Interior recommends specific house sizes to accommodate different bird species. We sized this birdhouse to fit chickadees and similar small nesting birds. If you desire to attract house wrens, make the entry hole 1" in diameter; for titmice, nuthatches, and downy woodpeckers, make it 1¼"; and for warblers, 1½" in diameter. Proper sizing of the entry hole will help keep larger, unwanted birds from moving in and taking over the house.

First, let's cut out the parts

1. Rip and crosscut two pieces of ¾"-thick stock (we used pine) to 7" wide and 10½" long for the front and back (A) blanks. (Since this project only requires a small amount of wood, we raided our scrap-wood bin to find the needed material.) Stack the front and back blanks together face-to-face using double-faced tape. Now, draw diagonal lines to find and mark the centerline on the face of your front piece.

2. Make a copy of the full-sized Front pattern found on *page 52*. (We made a photocopy.) Cut out the pattern, leaving a ¼–½" margin around all sides. Next, adhere your copy to the front piece, aligning the pattern's centerline with the centerline you just scribed on the front blank. (To adhere the pattern, we applied rubber cement sparingly on the pattern's back surface.)

3. Saw the front and back to shape. (As shown *above center*, we bandsawed the parts to shape, cutting just outside the pattern line. Then using our stationary belt

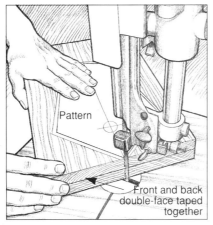
Front and back double-face taped together
Pattern

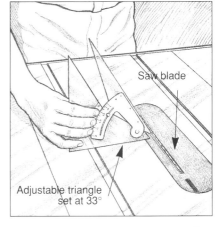
Saw blade
Adjustable triangle set at 33°

sander, we sanded each cut edge to the line.)

4. To make the sides, (B), crosscut a 13" length from 7¼"-wide and ¾"-thick stock. Next, tilt your saw blade to cut a 33° bevel. (As shown *above right*, we used an adjustable triangle to set the blade angle.) Bevel-rip one edge of the piece. Now, return the saw blade to vertical, lock the fence 6⅛" from the inside face of the blade, place the beveled edge of your piece against the fence, and then make the cut. Finally, crosscut two 6"-long sides from the piece.

5. For the birdhouse floor (C), select a piece of ¾"-thick stock that's at least 5" wide and 12" long. (We oversized this piece for safer cutting.) Next, tilt the saw blade to 12° from perpendicular. Bevel-rip one edge of the 12"-long piece. Now, bevel-rip the other edge, cutting it to a final width of 4⅜". Be sure to check the direction of the bevel on each edge before making any cuts. Now, crosscut a 4½"-long floor piece.

6. For the birdhouse roof (D), select a piece of ¾"-thick stock that's at least 7¼" wide and 21"

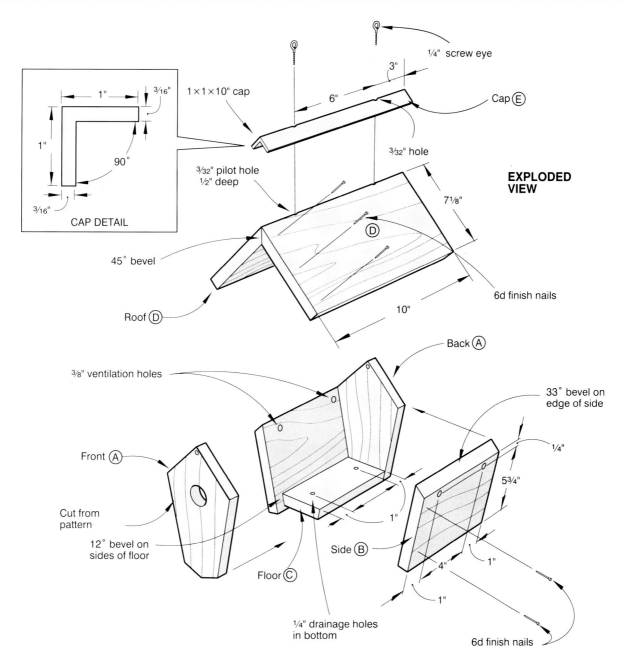

CAP DETAIL

1×1×10" cap

¼" screw eye

Cap Ⓔ

³⁄₃₂" pilot hole ½" deep

³⁄₃₂" hole

EXPLODED VIEW

45° bevel

Roof Ⓓ

7⅛"

6d finish nails

10"

Back Ⓐ

³⁄₈" ventilation holes

33° bevel on edge of side

Front Ⓐ

¼"

5¾"

Cut from pattern

12° bevel on sides of floor

Side Ⓑ

Floor Ⓒ

4"

1"

1"

1"

¼" drainage holes in bottom

6d finish nails

long. Tilt your saw blade to 45° from perpendicular, and bevel-cut one edge on the piece. Next, return the saw blade to perpendicular, and set the fence 7⅛" from the inside of the blade. Now, place the beveled edge of the piece against the rip fence, and rip it to width. Finally, crosscut two 10" lengths from this stock.

7. For the roof cap (E), crosscut a 10" length of 1" outside corner molding. (You can buy molding at homecenters. If you prefer to make your own cap, square a 12" length of 1¹⁄₁₆"-thick stock to 1". Next, saw the piece as dimensioned on the Cap detail *above,* and then crosscut it to the final length.)

Get ready to assemble and paint your birdhouse

1. Drill the ¼"-diameter vent holes through the floor, sides, and the front and back pieces where marked. Next, separate the front and back pieces, and bore the 1⅛"-diameter entry hole through the front. (We drilled all of the holes on our drill press.) Now, remove the pattern, and finish-sand all pieces.

2. Glue and nail the sides to the front and back. (We used Franklin's waterproof Titebond II glue and 6d finish nails.) Next, glue and nail the two roof pieces together. Center the roof on the house, and glue and nail it to the front and back. Set all nails. Glue the cap to the roof.

3. Place the floor piece inside the house, and turn it so it falls and wedges in place between the sides and front and back. Do not glue or nail the bottom. Sized correctly, it fits snugly in place, but allows you quick-and-easy access for cleaning.
continued

51

FLIGHT SCHOOL BIRDHOUSE
continued

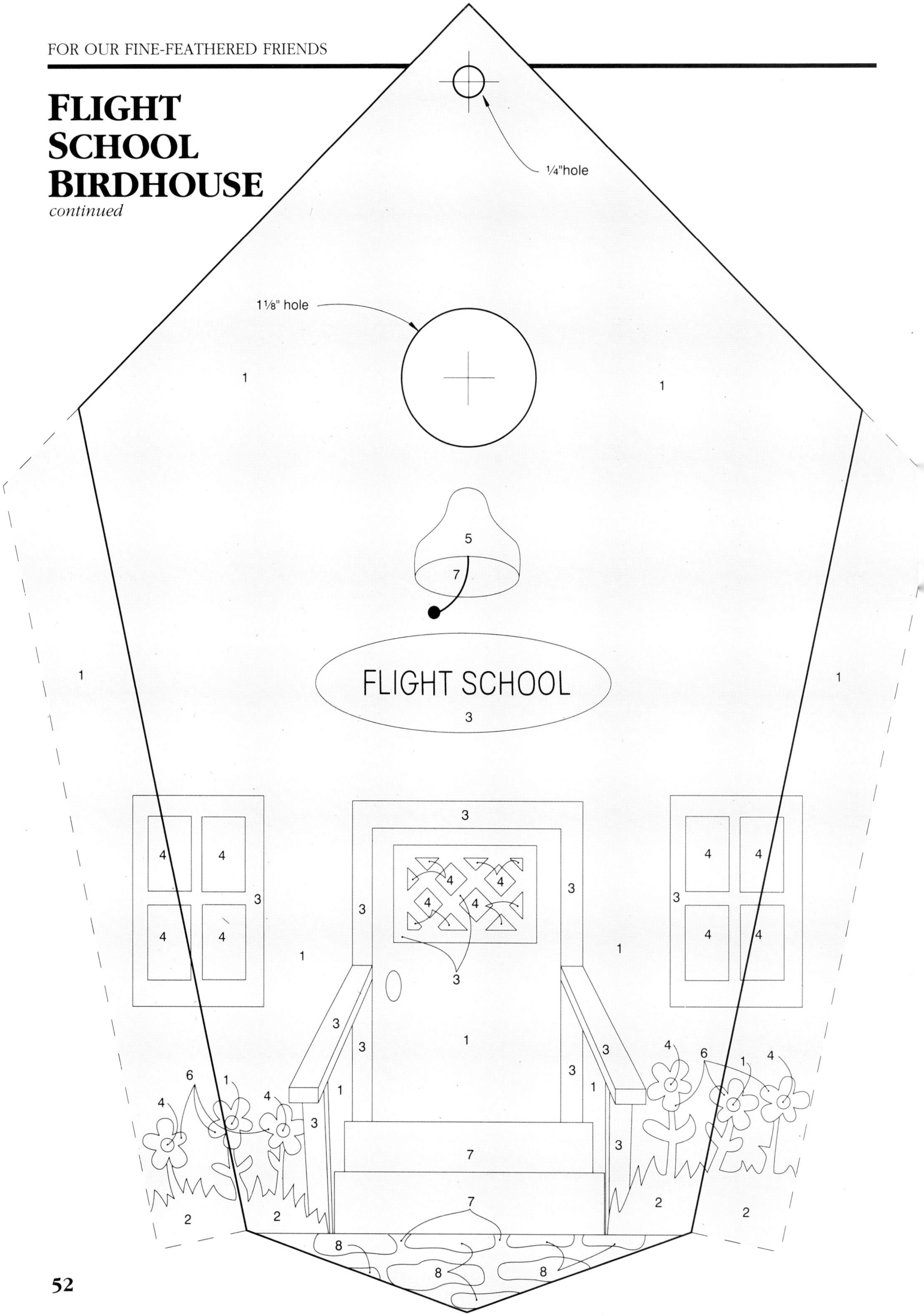

¼"hole

1⅛" hole

5

7

FLIGHT SCHOOL

3

1

1

1

1

1

1

3

3

3

3

3

3

3

4

4

4

4

4

4

4

4

4

4

4

4

4

4

4

4

3

3

3

3

3

1

1

1

1

3

3

3

3

3

3

7

7

7

6

6

1

1

4

4

4

2

2

2

2

8

8

8

Bill of Materials

Part	Finished Size*			Mat.	Qty.
	T	W	L		
A* front/back	¾"	6½"	10⅜"	P	2
B side	¾"	6⁹⁄₁₆"	6"	P	2
C floor	¾"	4³⁄₁₆"	4½"	P	1
D roof	¾"	7⅛"	10"	P	2
E cap	1"	1"	10"	P	1

*Cut parts marked with an * to final size using a pattern.

Material Key: P–pine
Supplies: 6d finish nails, ¼" screw eyes, chain or wire for hanging.

Color Key

1	Red
2	Green
3	White
4	Black
5	Gold
6	Yellow
7	Gray
8	Dark Gray

4. Finish your house as you wish. If you enjoy the whimsical look, and wish to paint your birdhouse like our Flight School model pictured on *page 50,* transfer the painting part of the pattern onto the front, sides and back. You can use carbon or transfer paper for this. Paint the Flight School version using our color scheme listed *above,* or create your own. If you prefer a simple paint job, use an exterior flat paint, and neutral colors such as gray, green, or light brown. You also may use exterior-grade wood stains and wood preservatives if you feel it needs additional protection. If you leave your house unfinished, the wood should eventually weather to a natural gray.

Tried-and-true tips to attract birds to your yard

• Houses of this type draw birds that normally nest in cavities or holes they find in the wild. You also may attract birds that nest in trees, shrubs, and vines if you place houses near these kinds of plants. We deliberately sized this house to appeal to small nesters. To attract larger birds, you'll need to increase the floor area, deepen the cavity, and enlarge the entry hole. For more information, check reference books at your public library.

• Despite what you remember from your childhood, birdhouses shouldn't have perches. In fact, ornithologists—the people who make a career out of studying birds—say perches invite predators, allowing them to reach in and destroy eggs or kill the newly hatched birds.

• You'll need to hang your birdhouse at specific heights in order to attract certain kinds of birds. For example, you'll discover chickadees and titmice typically nest between 6' and 15'

feet above the ground; warblers, 4-7', most wrens, 6-10', and downy woodpeckers, 6-20'. Hang your birdhouse within these height ranges. Watch for activity, and change the height if you don't see desirable occupants.

• Birds apparently prefer to have their houses mounted to something solid, such as a post or tree trunk. If you mount your birdhouse, make certain predators such as rats, cats, or squirrels cannot get to it. If you hang it from a tree limb, suspend it from two lines for better stability.

• Orient the house so the entry hole faces away from prevailing winds. Also, locate the house so it will be shaded from direct sun during the hot part of the day.

• Clean the house at the end of each brooding period, or when undesirable birds move in. This prevents litter buildup, helps protect the eggs, and also keeps down parasites. When you clean, check that all vent and drainage holes are open, too.

Note: *Do not paint or finish the interior of your birdhouse. If you finish the outside, let the application weather outdoors for about a month before moving it to a permanent location.*

5. To hang your birdhouse, drill ³⁄₃₂" pilot holes through the cap and ½" deep into the roof where marked. Turn a ¼" screw eye into each hole, and attach chains or wires to them. If you prefer to mount it to a post or tree, screw a 4"-wide mounting board to the back, and then attach it to your mounting post.

Project Tool List
Tablesaw
Bandsaw
Belt sander
Portable drill
Drill press
  Bits: ³⁄₃₂", ¼", ⅜", 1⅛"
Finishing sander

Note: *We built the project using the tools listed. You may be able to substitute other tools or equipment for listed items you don't have. Additional common hand tools and clamps may be required to complete the project.*

SHORT BRANCH SALOON FOR THE BIRDS

To get ready for the bird's return from their winter trip south, mosey down to your workshop right now to build this frontier-style saloon.

Note: *Sized for wrens, this decorator birdhouse includes ventilation and drain holes, and a bottom that comes off for cleaning. Hang or mount it 6–10' above the ground. If you mount it with the back against a solid surface, drill two ⅜" vent holes near the top of each side wall.*

1. Plane or resaw a 6x39" piece of cedar to ½" thick. You'll need a ¼" dowel 9" long, too. Cut the pieces for the Short Branch with your tablesaw, following the Cutting Diagram, *opposite.*

2. Rout a ½" rabbet ¼" deep on each inside edge of the front and back walls where shown on the Exploded View drawing. Temporarily assemble the front, back, and sides. With the bottoms even, mark each side wall at the front and back wall top corners. Disassemble, draw a line between the points on each side wall, and cut the angled tops. Drill the ⅞" hole in the front wall.

3. Now, draw the swinging door (see photograph) for woodburning. Draw the two lines at each side of the door about ¹⁄₁₆" apart. Space the horizontal louvers ⅛" apart. Draw 1½"x2¼" rectangles for the windows, dividing them into eight panes with ⅛" spacing. Place them ¾" from the bottom, ½" in from each edge on front and centered on each side.

4. Using our headline for your full-sized pattern, woodburn the sign. Then, add parallel vertical lines about ¼" apart on the front, back, and sides (except around the lettering). Woodburn floorboards on the porch and shingles on the porch roof.

5. Drill ¼" dowel holes and drain holes through the base and ¾" vent holes through the back wall where shown. Cut two ¼" dowels 4¼" long and sand a 45° angle on one end of each.

6. Now, glue the four walls, roof, and porch roof together. Attach the bottom with screws, but no glue. Insert the dowels from the bottom, pushing them up to meet the porch roof. Glue them to the base, but not to the porch roof, and then cut them off flush with the bottom of the base.

7. Apply a clear, outdoor finish (we used Thompson's Water Seal) before opening the Short Branch for business.

Project Tool List
Tablesaw
Router
    ½" rabbet bit
Portable drill
Drill press
    Bits: ⁹⁄₆₄", ¼", ¾", 1⅛"
Finishing sander
Woodburning tool

EXPLODED VIEW

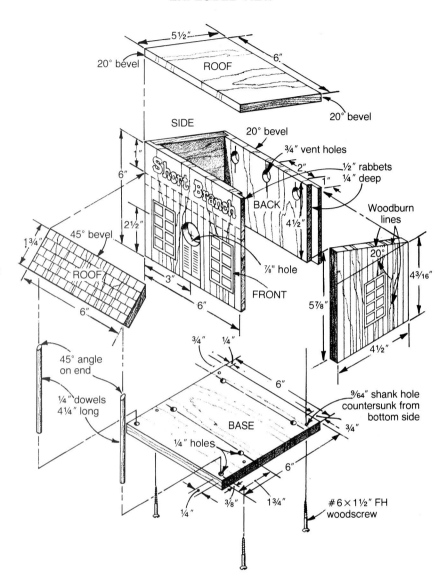

CUTTING DIAGRAM

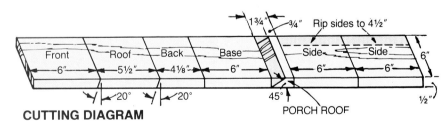

Note: We built the project using the tools listed. You may be able to substitute other tools or equipment for listed items you don't have. Additional common hand tools and clamps may be required to complete the project.

STARS-AND-STRIPES WREN HOUSE

John Dennis, contributing editor to *Bird Watcher's Digest,* offers the following advice concerning perches: DON'T include them! A bird can easily land on the entrance hole and go into the nesting box from there. Decorating your birdhouse with a perch provides birds such as sparrows and starlings a vantage point from which they can take over the house for themselves. These mischievous birds have been known to destroy the eggs or kill the young nesting inside.

1. To make the front and back (A), start by cutting a piece of ¾" stock to 5½" wide by 14" long, bevel-ripping the edges at 45°. Next, cut two 6½"-long pieces from this board. Place these two pieces on a flat surface, beveled edges down, and lay out the roofline on each (see the Exploded View drawing for dimensions). Make the roof cuts.

2. For the sides (B), cut a piece of ¾" stock to 6" wide by 8" long, bevel-ripping the edges at 45°. From this piece, cut the sides to their 3¾" finished length.

3. Using ½" stock, cut the roof pieces (C) to 7¼" wide by 6" long. Bevel one end of each for a 5" finished length. Transfer the full-sized star pattern to ¼" stock, and cut the two stars to shape.

4. Drill three ⅜" ventilation holes in the back piece and a 1⅛" entrance hole (sized for wrens) in the front. With the bottom edges flush, glue and nail the sides between the front and back pieces. Measure the opening, and cut the bottom (D) to size, less 1/16" in length and width. (We made the bottom slightly smaller than the opening, and installed it with screws to make it removable for annual cleaning.) Drill a ¼" drainage hole in each corner of the bottom piece. Drill the shank and pilot holes, and screw the bottom in place.

5. Paint the house and two wooden stars antique white and the roof soldier blue. Allow the paint to dry. To paint the stripes on the side pieces, adhere masking tape to the birdhouse, spacing the tape equally apart. Paint the stripes barn red. Transfer the full-sized small star patterns to the house front and paint them soldier blue.

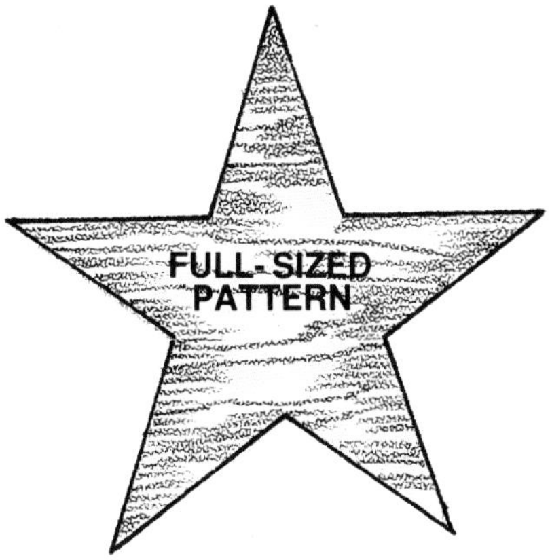

FULL-SIZED
PATTERN

6. Nail the roof pieces to the assembled house. To age the house, lightly sand the edges. Apply medium walnut stain to the birdhouse, and immediately wipe off most of it. Nail the stars to the one side of the roof.

Project Tool List
Tablesaw
Portable drill
Drill press
Bits: 7/64", 5/32", ¼", ⅜", 1⅛"
Finishing sander

Note: *We built the project using the tools listed. You may be able to substitute other tools or equipment for listed items you don't have. Additional common hand tools and clamps may be required to complete the project.*

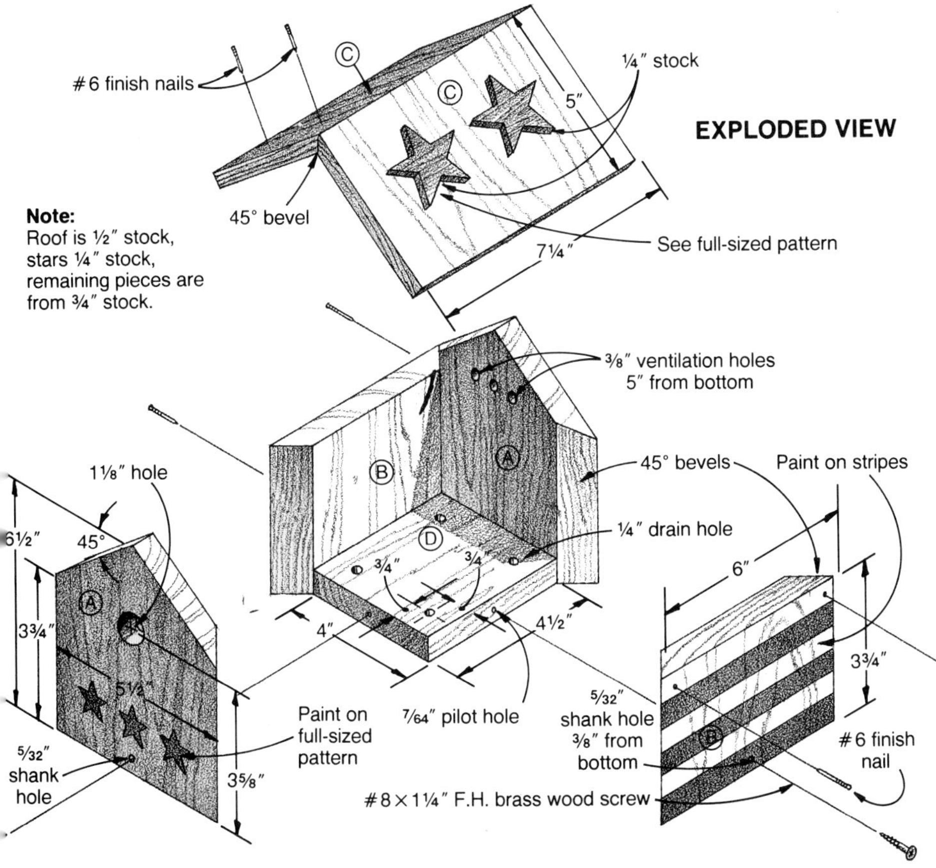

EXPLODED VIEW
#6 finish nails
¼" stock
5"
45° bevel
7¼"
See full-sized pattern
Note:
Roof is ½" stock,
stars ¼" stock,
remaining pieces are
from ¾" stock.
⅜" ventilation holes
5" from bottom
45° bevels
Paint on stripes
¼" drain hole
1⅛" hole
6½"
45°
3¾"
5½"
¾"
4"
4½"
6"
3¾"
5/32" shank hole
3⅝"
Paint on full-sized pattern
7/64" pilot hole
5/32" shank hole ⅜" from bottom
#6 finish nail
#8 × 1¼" F.H. brass wood screw

HUMDINGER OF A FEEDER

We hope you'll agree that hovering creatures as fascinating as hummingbirds deserve to drink from a fancy feeder. This clever design fills the bill, and also shields the sugar-laced water from harsh sun rays that can spoil the solution. Don't miss this chance to build a handsome feeding station for your busy backyard visitors.

Make and assemble the simple feeder box

1. Cut a piece of ¾"-thick stock measuring at least 3½x14". (We used redwood from our scrap bin, but cedar or pine also would work.) Next, resaw two ¼"-thick strips from the piece. (We resawed the material on our tablesaw.) Sand the cut surfaces on both pieces to remove any saw marks. Now, rip

and crosscut four walls (A) to the dimensions listed on the Bill of Materials on *page 61.*

Note: After our tiny friends took off for the winter, we did some remodeling. Although you won't see them on the feeder shown in the photo, we added viewing slots in two opposite side walls. The slots make it easier to tell how much syrup remains in the bottle.

2. To form the slots in two box walls, first scribe a centerline on one wall piece. Mark points ⅝" and 3⅝" from the bottom on this centerline. Stack the marked wall piece on top of a second, and drill a ¼" hole through the centerpoint nearest the bottom. Separate the wall pieces. Next, chuck a ¼" straight bit in your table-mounted router and place the hole of the wall piece over the bit. Clamp a fence against the right side of the piece, and then push the piece forward to rout the 3"-long slot as shown *opposite.* Rout a slot in the second wall piece the same way.

3. To make the triangular corners (B) shown on the Corner detail *far right,* plane or resaw a ¾"-thick piece of stock measuring at least 2x 12" to ½" thick. Angle your table-saw blade to 45°, and bevel-rip the piece down the middle. Return the blade perpendicular to the table, and then carefully rip a ½"-wide triangular strip from the edge on both pieces. Crosscut two 5¾" lengths from each of these pieces.

4. Dry-fit the walls as shown on the Exploded View drawing *opposite,* noting how the wall edges lap and that the slotted walls are opposite each other. Now, using waterproof glue, adhere a triangular corner to each wall, aligning it with the outside edge and the bottom. (We used two-part resorcinol glue, but epoxy or waterproof TiteBond II also would work.) After the adhesive sets, glue the four walls together to form the 2⅞x2⅞" box. Use tape or rubber bands to hold *continued*

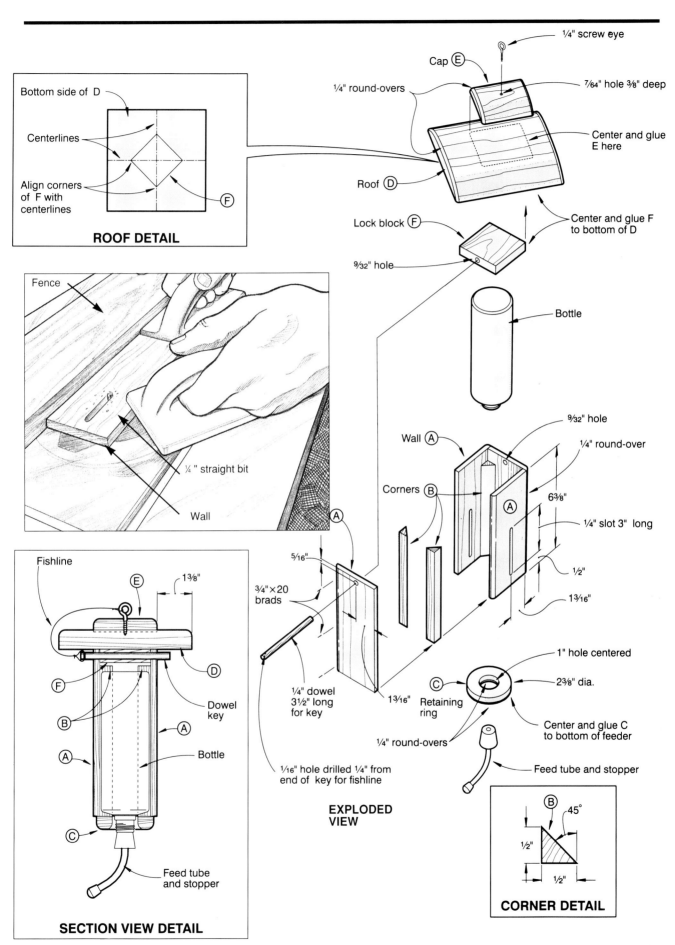

ROOF DETAIL

Bottom side of D

Centerlines

Align corners of F with centerlines

F

CORNER DETAIL

B

45°

½"

½"

SECTION VIEW DETAIL

Fishline

E

1⅜"

F

B

A

A

C

Dowel key

D

Bottle

Feed tube and stopper

EXPLODED VIEW

¼" screw eye

Cap E

¼" round-overs

⁷⁄₆₄" hole ⅜" deep

Center and glue E here

Roof D

Lock block F

⁹⁄₃₂" hole

Center and glue F to bottom of D

Bottle

⁹⁄₃₂" hole

¼" round-over

Wall A

Corners B

6⅜"

A

¼" slot 3" long

½"

1³⁄₁₆"

A

5⁄₁₆"

¾"×20 brads

¼" dowel 3½" long for key

1³⁄₁₆"

Retaining ring

C

1" hole centered

2⅜" dia.

Center and glue C to bottom of feeder

¼" round-overs

Feed tube and stopper

1⁄₁₆" hole drilled ¼" from end of key for fishline

Fence

¼" straight bit

Wall

59

HUMDINGER OF A FEEDER
continued

the pieces temporarily, and then drive ¾"×20 brads.

5. For the retaining ring (C), rip and crosscut a ½"-thick piece of stock to 3×6". Using a holesaw, cut a 2⅝" diameter disc from the piece. Bore a 1"-diameter hole through the center of the disc. Now, rout a ¼" round-over around one outside edge. (To rout the edge of this small disc, we first inserted a 1" dowel into the hole. Then we clamped it in a vise as shown at *right.*)

6. Center the retaining ring on the bottom of the feeder box, and then glue it in place. After the glue sets, rout the inside edge of the hole, using a ¼"-piloted round-over bit. (We clamped the box in a vise with the ring facing up, and then routed around the inside of the hole.)

Build the roof in three parts

1. Make copies of the roof (D) and cap (E) patterns on *page 61* and cut them to shape. (We traced ours using carbon paper.) Next, rip and crosscut a ¾"-thick piece of stock to 5¾" wide and 5¼" long. Apply adhesive to the back of your roof pattern, and adhere it to one end of the piece. Bandsaw the curved edges, following the pattern profile. (As shown at *right,* we adhered the roof blank to a 10" length of 2×4 with double-faced tape, and then used it to hold the part vertical while sawing it to shape.) Remove the pattern.

2. Cut a piece of ½"-thick stock to 3" wide and 2½" long. Adhere the cap pattern to one end. Bandsaw it to shape, following the techniques you used to form the roof.

3. To make the lock block (F), rip and crosscut a ½"-thick square to fit inside the top of the feeder box. Allow some clearance so it can be removed easily. (Ours measures 2⅟₁₆" square.)

4. Mark the hole centerpoint for the ¼" dowel key on the feeder wall where shown on the Exploded View drawing. Adhere the lock

Retaining ring

Insert 1"-dia. dowel to hold ring for routing

block to a piece of wood with double-faced tape. Now, as shown *opposite top,* insert the lock block into the top of the feeder, and drill a ⁹⁄₃₂" hole through both walls and the lock block. (While drilling, we placed scrap under the feeder box to avoid chip-out.)

5. Sand the roof parts and round over the edges where instructed on the Exploded View drawing. (We used 100- and 120-grit sandpaper.) Round over the four edges on the feeder walls. (We sanded them on our belt sander.) Do not rout the edges because of the brads.

6. Center, glue, and clamp the cap to the top of the roof where shown on the Section View and Exploded View drawings. Next, center, glue, and clamp the lock block to the underside of the roof, orienting the lock block 90° to the roof axis where shown on the Roof detail on *page 59.* Drill a ⁷⁄₆₄" pilot hole ⅜"-deep into the cap center where shown, and then turn a ¼" screw eye into it.

7. For the key, crosscut a 3½" length of ¼" dowel. Drill a ⅟₁₆" hole through the key. Tie one end of a

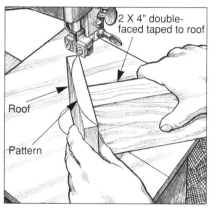

2 X 4" double-faced taped to roof

Roof

Pattern

12" length of fishline through the dowel and the other end to the screw eye in the roof. This will keep the key from getting lost. To test-fit your feeder, fill the bottle with water and slide it inside. (See the Buying Guide, *opposite,* for a mail-order source of the feeder parts.) Insert the lock block into the top of the feeder so the holes align, and then push the dowel key through the hole to lock the roof and box together.

8. You may apply a wood preservative to the wood parts if you desire. However, a preservative

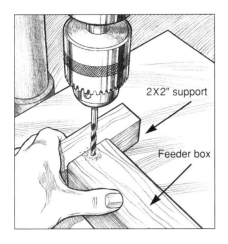

2X2" support

Feeder box

isn't necessary on redwood or cedar; when left unfinished, these woods weather to an attractive gray color.

9. Place the bottle in your feeder, fill it with your hummingbird syrup mixture, wet the stopper, and insert it firmly into the bottle opening. To avoid dripping, always fill the bottle completely full before pushing in the stopper. (A small amount of dripping—a drop every 3 or 4 hours—is unavoidable.)

Now, turn the feeder over, lock on the roof, and hang. If possible, place your feeder in a shady location and out of the wind. For more information on enticing and feeding hummingbird, read the tips *below.*

Buying Guide

• **Hummingbird feeder kit.** Three plastic bottles, feed tubes, and stoppers. Kit #1225. For current prices and shipping costs contact Meisel Hardware Specialties, P.O. Box 70W, Mound, MN 55364-0070. Or call 800/441-9870 or 612/471-8550 to order.

Project Tool List

Tablesaw
Bandsaw
Router
  Router table
  Bits: ¼" straight, ¼" round-over
Drill press
  Bits: ¹⁄₁₆", ⁷⁄₆₄", ¼", ⁹⁄₃₂", 1"
  Holesaw, 2⅜"
Belt sander
Finishing sander

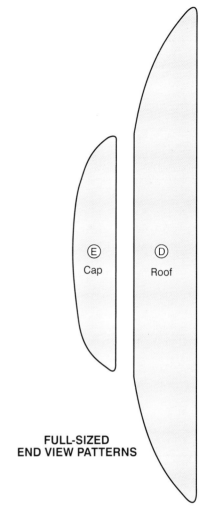

Ⓔ
Cap

Ⓓ
Roof

FULL-SIZED
END VIEW PATTERNS

How to attract hummingbirds to your yard

• You can buy prepared hummingbird food mixtures at many stores selling bird food, or you can make your own. One widely used recipe calls for boiling 8 ounces of water for several minutes, and then dissolving 1½ to 2 ounces (3.5:1.5 or 4:1 ratio) of white sugar in the water. Add a few drops of red food coloring if you wish. Cool the mixture. You can store the excess syrup for a few days in a refrigerator. Bird experts advise against substituting honey, corn syrups, or artificial sweeteners for the sugar.

• Thoroughly clean the feeder parts before the first filling. Then, clean the feeder bottle and feed tube every three or four days with a hot water and vinegar solution. Do not use soap. Rinse parts with clean water and refill the bottle.

• If bees, wasps, or ants become a nuisance, you can try fashioning a small hardware-cloth screen around the tip. This should keep bees and wasps from the tip, but still allow the hummingbirds access to it. Some commercially available syrups have an ingredient reported to keep bees and wasps away from the feeder. If ants invade your feeder, try hanging it on monofilament (fishing) line, or consider buying a product called Ant-Scat.

• You will have better luck attracting hummingbirds to your yard if you have flowering plants in the area. Impatiens, fuchsia, flowering quince, hollyhock, honeysuckle, azalea, citrus trees, trumpet vine, and other nectar-rich flowering plants provile natural food for hummingbirds. The birds rely on these nectar sources for their main diet and will supplement it with syrup from a feeder.

Bill of Materials

Part	Finished Size*			Mat.	Qty.
	T	W	L		
A wall	¼"	2⅜"	6⅜"	R	4
B corner	½"	½"	5¾"	R	4
C ring	½"	2⅜" dia.		R	1
D roof	¾"	5⅛"	5¼"	R	1
E cap	½"	2½"	2½"	R	1
F lock block	½"	2¹⁄₁₆"	2¹⁄₁₆"	R	1

Material Key: R—redwood
Supplies: ¼" dowel, ¾"X20 brads, ¼" screw eye, 1¾X6¼" (8-oz. capacity) plastic bottle, rubber stopper, feed tube, fishline.

Note: *We built the project using the tools listed. You may be able to substitute other tools or equipment for listed items you don't have. Additional common hand tools and clamps may be required to complete the project.*

ACORNY KIND OF BIRDHOUSE

If chickadees or wrens could talk (they do, of course, but not in our language), they'd thank you for this not-so-humble domicile. We've included everything a bird desires—nesting space, ventilation, and drainage—and omitted a perch at the advice of bird experts. Here's one nut you won't mind hanging around the yard.

Cut the pieces and form the lamination

1. From 2×10 stock (we used spruce), cut five pieces measuring 7 ½×11½" for parts A, B, and C. Now, as dimensioned on the Lamination Drawing, lay out the openings in parts B and C. Drill a ⅜" blade-start hole, and cut each opening to shape with a jigsaw.

2. With the edges and ends flush, glue and clamp the five pieces. Let the glue dry overnight.

Note: *For joints that will stand up to the extremes of Mother Nature, use Titebond II water-resistant glue, slow-set epoxy, or resorcinol glue.*

Make the template and turn the acorn to shape

1. Cut a piece of poster board to 6×12". Starting at the bottom, draw a 1" grid on the paper. Lay out the shape of half of the birdhouse on the marked grid, using the Grid Half Pattern as a guide. To do this, mark the points where the pattern outline crosses each grid line. Draw lines to connect the points. Cut the template to shape.

2. Draw diagonals on both ends of the birdhouse lamination to find centers. Using a center punch and a mallet, make an indentation at each marked centerpoint.

3. For ease in turning round, use a compass to draw a 7½"-diameter circle on one end of the lamination. Then, chamfer each corner of the

lamination, cutting outside of the marked circle.

4. Mount the lamination between centers, centering the headstock and tailstock points at the indented centerpoints.

5. With a 1" gouge, turn the lamination round. Now, turn the lamination to shape, using the template as a guide. Turn the top and bottom of the acorn last; you'll want plenty of stock at both ends when turning the profile to shape. (We used a 1" and a ½" gouge, as well as a parting tool, to do the shaping.) For a natural texture, we left our project rough and did not sand it.

Drill the entrance hole and cut off the lid

1. As shown in the photo at *right,* clamp the spur center with a handscrew clamp. Position the

bottom of the clamp on the lathe bed to prevent the acorn from turning. Drill a 1⅛" hole where dimensioned on the Grid Half Pattern.

2. Using a handsaw, cut the cap from the nut as shown in the photo *opposite.* (To prevent the saw from binding, we made a few cuts, loosened the clamp, and rotated

Clamp the spur center to hold the birdhouse firmly in position, and drill a 1⅛" hole into the cavity.

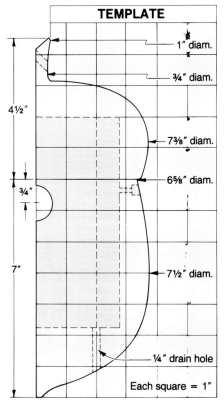

TEMPLATE

1" diam.

¾" diam.

4½"

7⅜" diam.

¾"

6⅝" diam.

7"

7½" diam.

¼" drain hole

Each square = 1"

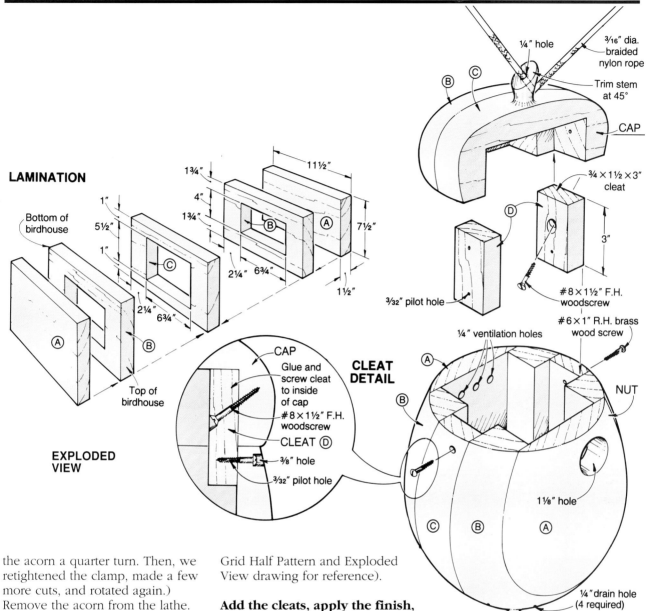

LAMINATION

Bottom of birdhouse

Top of birdhouse

EXPLODED VIEW

1¾"
11½"
4"
1¾"
1"
5½"
1"
7½"
2¼" 6¾"
1½"
2¼" 6¾"

Ⓐ Ⓑ Ⓒ

¾×1½×3" cleat

3"

3/32" pilot hole

#8×1½" F.H. woodscrew

#6×1" R.H. brass wood screw

¼" hole

3/16" dia. braided nylon rope

Trim stem at 45°

CAP

Ⓑ Ⓒ Ⓓ

¼" ventilation holes

NUT

1⅛" hole

¼" drain hole (4 required)

CLEAT DETAIL

CAP

Glue and screw cleat to inside of cap

#8×1½" F.H. woodscrew

CLEAT Ⓓ

⅜" hole

3/32" pilot hole

the acorn a quarter turn. Then, we retightened the clamp, made a few more cuts, and rotated again.) Remove the acorn from the lathe. Finish making the cut to separate the cap from the nut. Cut the stem at a 45° angle, and drill a ¼" hole through the stem for the rope.

3. Drill three ¼" ventilation holes and four ¼" drainage holes (see the

Grid Half Pattern and Exploded View drawing for reference).

Add the cleats, apply the finish, and hang

1. Cut two cleats (D) to ¾×1½×3". Glue and screw them to the inside of the cap (see the Exploded View drawing and accompanying Cleat Detail for reference). Let the glue dry overnight.

2. To attach the cap, position the cap on the nut and drill the two holes as dimensioned on the Cleat Detail. Fasten the cap to the nut.

3. Finish the outside but not the inside of the birdhouse. (We stained the cap, and then applied two coats of clear water sealant to both the cap and the nut.)

4. Run a 3/16"-diameter braided nylon rope through the hole and hang from a limb. To prevent the birdhouse from spinning in the

wind, double the rope as shown in the opening photograph and on the Exploded View drawing.

Project Tool List
Tablesaw
Jigsaw
Lathe
  Turning gouges, parting tool
Portable drill
  Bits: 3/32", ¼", ⅜", 1⅛"

Note: *We built the project using the tools listed. You may be able to substitute other tools or equipment for listed items you don't have. Additional common hand tools and clamps may be required to complete the project.*

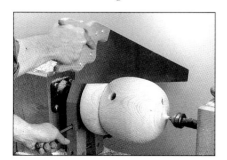

Using a handsaw, make cuts all the way around the laminated turning to separate the cap from the nut.

HOUSE DRESSING

Outdoor accessories can give your house pizzazz. The projects here include a flower wagon, a golf-inspired whirligig, two handsome planters, landscape lighting fixtures, a party-time cart, and a welcoming number sign.

BLOOMIN'-GOOD WAGON

Roll into summer with a patio accessory reminiscent of yesteryear's flower wagons. In addition to boosting your floral displays, we imagine some of you probably will load its 16"-long wagon box with rolls or chips for your next barbecue.

Let's start by building the wagon's undercarriage

1. Rip and crosscut two 10" lengths of 2×4. (Because we planned to paint our wagon, we chose pine lumber.) Copy the Axle pattern on *page 69*. (We photocopied ours.) Trace the axle outline and the end-hole centerlines onto the face of both axle blanks. Next, using a try square, transfer the axle-hole centerlines from the face to the ends on each 2×4. Now, mark the centerpoints for these ½" holes, and then drill them 1¼" deep into the 2×4 ends.

2. Cut the ⅜"-deep, 2"-wide notch in the top of one axle where indicated on the pattern. (We cut out this notch on our tablesaw.) Now, bandsaw both axles (A) to shape. Sand the cut edges with 100-grit sandpaper. (We used a 2"-diameter sanding drum chucked into our drill press.)

3. Rip and crosscut the wagon platform (B) as dimensioned on the Bill of Materials. See the Cutting Diagram on *page 66* for how we laid out our wood. If you don't have 10"-wide stock for the platform and wheels, edge-glue narrower pieces.

Note: *For joints that will stand up to the extremes of Mother Nature, use Titebond II water-resistant glue, slow-set epoxy, or resorcinol glue.*

4. Prepare a full-sized wheel pattern. (We made two copies of the half pattern on *page 69,* then aligned and taped them together.) Using carbon paper, trace four wheel outlines onto your wide stock. Bore the ½"-center holes where marked, and then saw the wheels (C) to shape. (First we bored ⅞₆"- and ½"-diameter holes in each wheel segment to preshape the inside corners. Then, we scrollsawed the areas between the spokes and bandsawed the outside edge, cutting just wide of the line.)

5. Sand all sawed edges to the line on the four wheels. Round over all cut edges on both sides of each wheel. (We used a piloted ¼" round-over bit in our router.)

6. Rip and crosscut a piece of ¾"-thick pine to 2×7". Resaw it to ⅜" thick for the wagon tongue (F) Finish-sand the piece, and then bore the ¾" hole where shown.

Lots of drawings will help you make the wagon box

1. From ¾ ×5½" stock, crosscut two 10"-long end (D) blanks, and then two 17"-long side (E) blanks.

2. Set up your tablesaw as shown on the Step 1 drawing *above right*. You'll make the miter- and bevel-cuts shown on the Box Parts drawing on *page 67*. Our drawings at *right* show the setup on a tablesaw with a right-tilting blade. If your saw's arbor tilts left, set up the fence and miter-cut on the *opposite* side. Now, cut the beveled-miter on one end of the box ends and sides as shown *below*.

continued

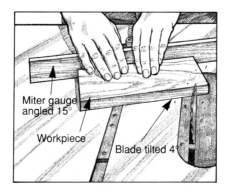

Miter gauge angled 15°
Workpiece
Blade tilted 4°

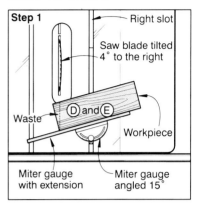

Step 1
Right slot
Saw blade tilted 4° to the right
Waste
D and E
Workpiece
Miter gauge with extension
Miter gauge angled 15°

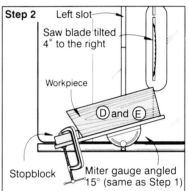

Step 2
Left slot
Saw blade tilted 4° to the right
Workpiece
D and E
Stopblock
Miter gauge angled 15° (same as Step 1)

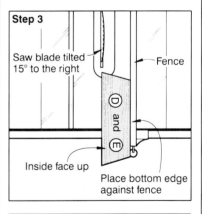

Step 3
Saw blade tilted 15° to the right
Fence
D and E
Inside face up
Place bottom edge against fence

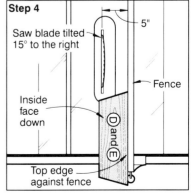

Step 4
Saw blade tilted 15° to the right
5"
Fence
Inside face down
D and E
Top edge against fence

BLOOMIN'-GOOD WAGON

continued

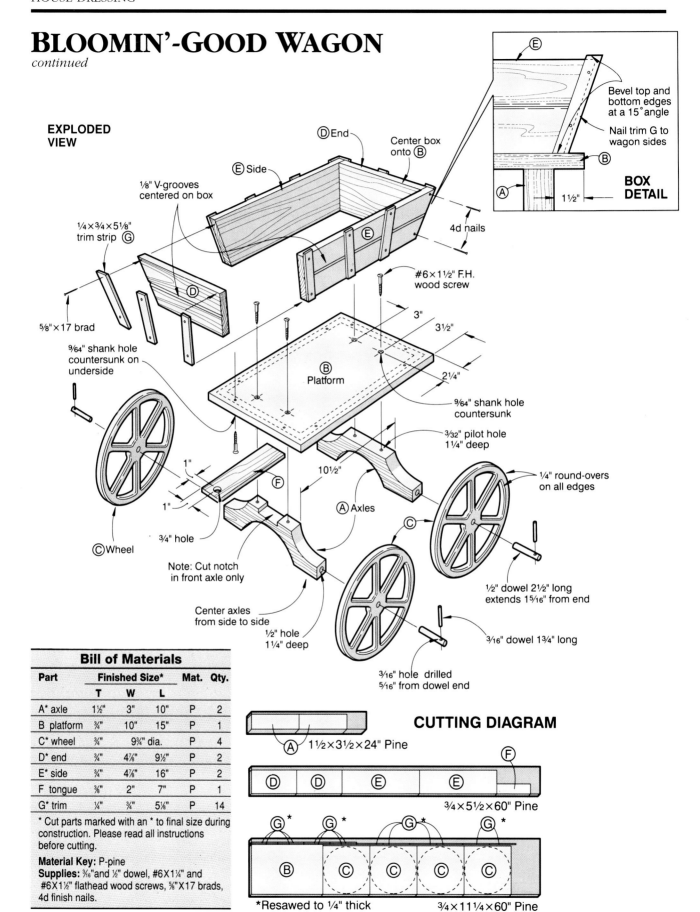

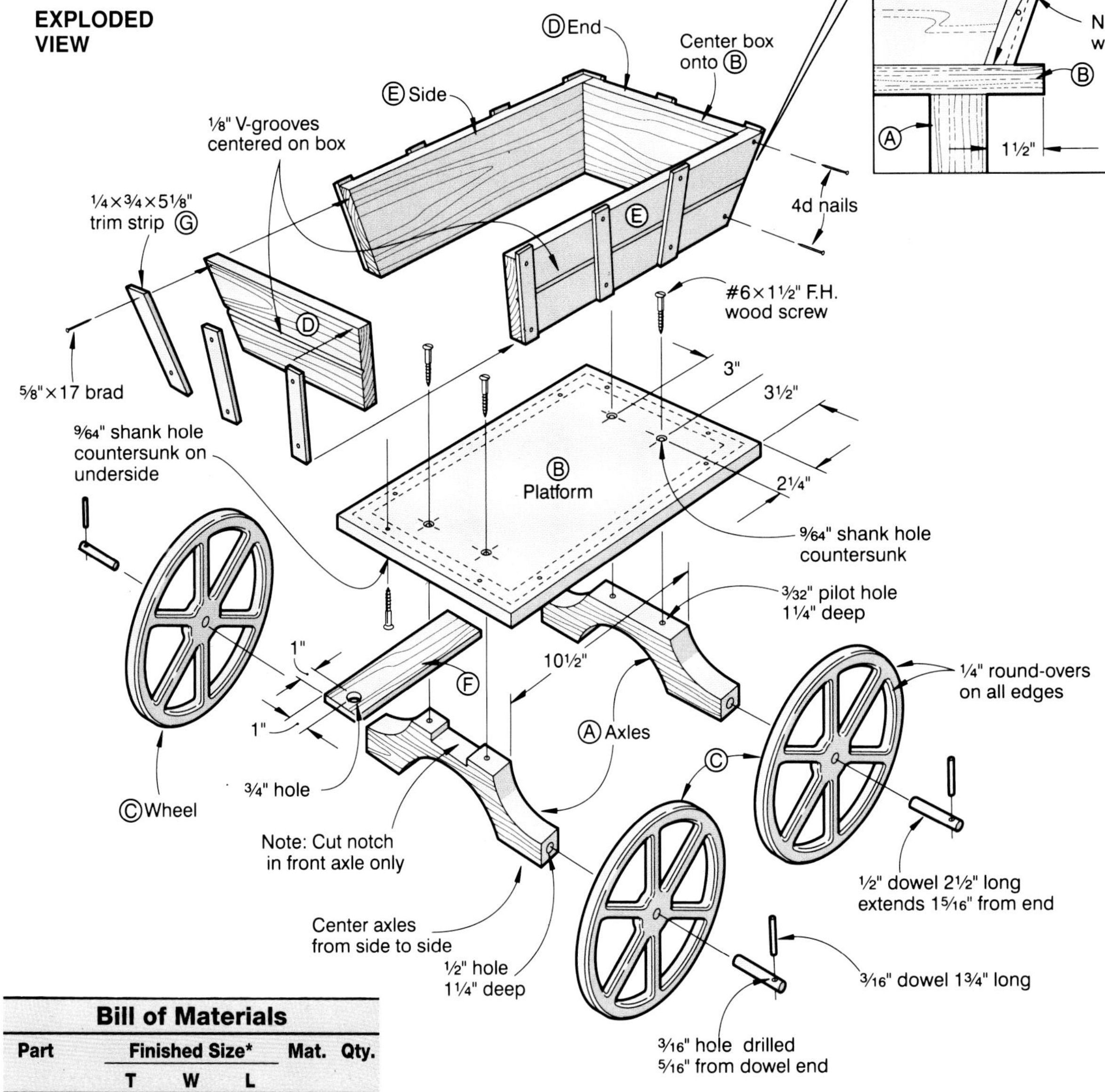
EXPLODED VIEW
Ⓓ End
Center box onto Ⓑ
Ⓔ Side
1/8" V-grooves centered on box
1/4×3/4×5 1/8" trim strip Ⓖ
4d nails
Ⓔ
Ⓓ
#6×1 1/2" F.H. wood screw
5/8"×17 brad
9/64" shank hole countersunk on underside
3"
3 1/2"
Ⓑ Platform
2 1/4"
9/64" shank hole countersunk
3/32" pilot hole 1 1/4" deep
1"
10 1/2"
1/4" round-overs on all edges
1"
Ⓕ
Ⓐ Axles
Ⓒ
3/4" hole
Ⓒ Wheel
Note: Cut notch in front axle only
1/2" dowel 2 1/2" long extends 1 5/16" from end
Center axles from side to side
1/2" hole 1 1/4" deep
3/16" dowel 1 3/4" long
3/16" hole drilled 5/16" from dowel end

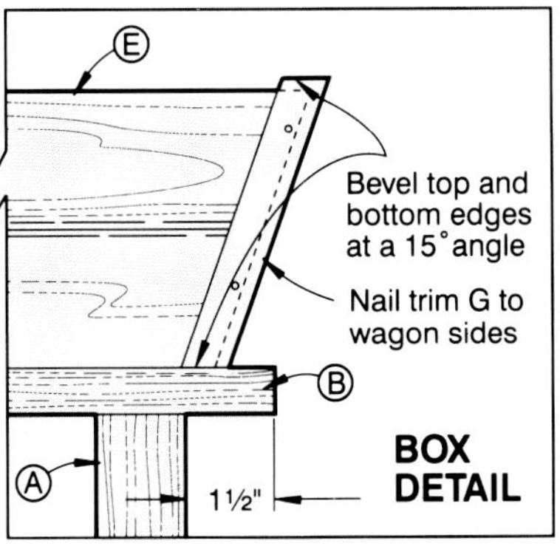
Ⓔ
Bevel top and bottom edges at a 15° angle
Nail trim G to wagon sides
Ⓑ
Ⓐ
1 1/2"
BOX DETAIL

Bill of Materials					
Part	Finished Size*			Mat.	Qty.
	T	W	L		
A* axle	1½"	3"	10"	P	2
B platform	¾"	10"	15"	P	1
C* wheel	¾"	9¾" dia.		P	4
D* end	¾"	4⅞"	9½"	P	2
E* side	¾"	4⅞"	16"	P	2
F tongue	⅜"	2"	7"	P	1
G* trim	¼"	¾"	5⅛"	P	14

* Cut parts marked with an * to final size during construction. Please read all instructions before cutting.

Material Key: P-pine

Supplies: 3/16" and ½" dowel, #6X1¼" and #6X1½" flathead wood screws, ⅝"X17 brads, 4d finish nails.

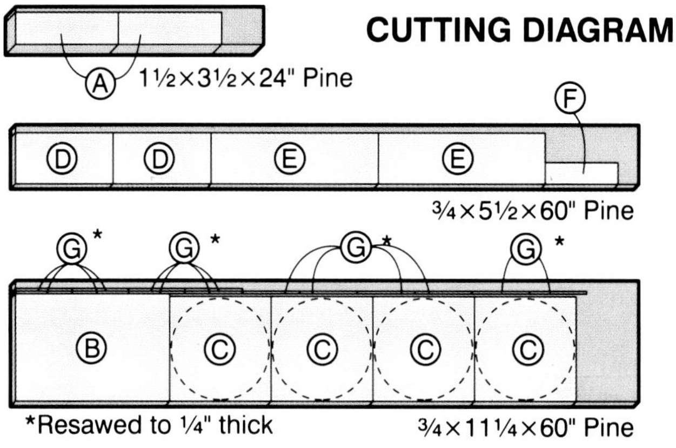
CUTTING DIAGRAM
Ⓐ 1 1/2×3 1/2×24" Pine
Ⓕ
Ⓓ Ⓓ Ⓔ Ⓔ
3/4×5 1/2×60" Pine
Ⓖ* Ⓖ* Ⓖ* Ⓖ*
Ⓑ Ⓒ Ⓒ Ⓒ Ⓒ
*Resawed to 1/4" thick
3/4×11 1/4×60" Pine

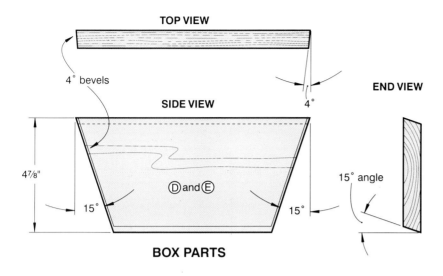

TOP VIEW

4° bevels

SIDE VIEW

4°

END VIEW

4⅞"

15°   Ⓓ and Ⓔ   15°

15° angle

BOX PARTS

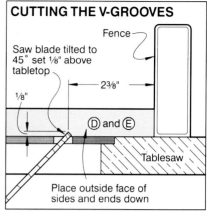

CUTTING THE V-GROOVES

Fence

Saw blade tilted to 45° set ⅛" above tabletop

2⅜"

⅛"

Ⓓ and Ⓔ

Tablesaw

Place outside face of sides and ends down

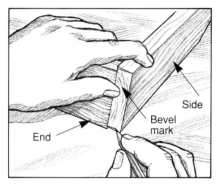

Side

Bevel mark

End

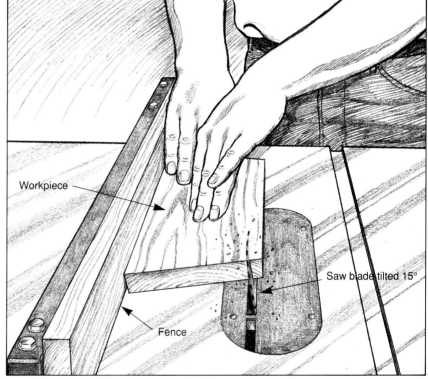

Workpiece

Fence

Saw blade tilted 15°

3. To bevel-miter the opposite end of each piece, set up the saw as shown on the Step 2 drawing on *page 65.* Do not change blade angle or miter setting—simply move your miter gauge to the left slot. Next, mark the final lengths on the top edge of one end (9½") and one side (16") piece. Place the bottom edge of this marked end against the miter gauge, align the mark with the blade, and then clamp a stopblock to the miter-gauge extension. Bevel-miter the second end on both end pieces. Now, reset the stopblock to accommodate the 16"-long sides, and bevel-miter the second end on them.

4. It's easy to get confused making the next two cuts, so we suggest you dry-assemble the box to mate the beveled corners. Check the corners for square, and then mark the inside faces, and letter the mating corners, A-A, B-B, C-C, and D-D. As shown *above,* mark the

ends to indicate the direction for top and bottom bevels.

5. To bevel-rip the top edges on the box sides and ends, set up your saw as shown on the Step 3 drawing. Position the fence so you can make a full bevel-rip along the top edge. Turn the inside face up and place the bottom (narrowest) edge against the fence. Make sure the bevel will angle in the same direction as the line you scribed across the end of the piece in the

previous step. Now, bevel-rip the top edge on all four box pieces.

6. Set up your tablesaw as shown on the Step 4 drawing on *page 65.* Place the top edge against the fence as shown *above,* with the *inside* face down. Again, check that the bevel angles the same direction as your scribed line. Now, bevel-rip the bottom edge on all box pieces.

7. To form the V-groove, set your saw as shown on the Cutting the V-Grooves drawing *top right.* Mark
continued

67

BLOOMIN'-GOOD WAGON
continued

the center on the edge of one box piece, and align it with the blade. Position the fence against the piece and lock it in place. Now, placing the *outside* face down and the top edge against the fence, saw the groove in all box pieces.

8. Glue and nail the box together. (We started the nails in the sides, and applied Franklin's Titebond II waterproof glue along the edges of the box ends. For easy nailing, we clamped each end in a vise, aligned the edges of the sides on it, and finished driving the nails.) Square the box corners, and clamp if necessary to hold it square until the glue dries.

Order the flowers—you're nearly finished

1. Glue the tongue in the front axle's notch. Next, cut four 2½" lengths of ½" dowel. Drill a ³⁄₁₆" hole through each of them ⁵⁄₁₆" from the end. Glue these ½" dowels in the axle holes, letting them extend 1⁵⁄₁₆" out from the end. Next, center the axles on the underside of the platform where shown on the Exploded View drawing on *page 66.* Square them to the platform, and then clamp both in place temporarily. Now, drill and countersink the shank and pilot holes where dimensioned, and then screw both axles to the platform.

2. Center the box on top of the platform. Scribe a line along the inside edges of the box sides. Next, use these lines as a guide to locate two ⁹⁄₆₄" shank holes on both sides. (We centered these holes ⅜" outside the lines.) Now, drill these holes from the top down through the platform, angling them inward at 15°. Finally, countersink them on the underside of the platform.

3. Position the box on top of the platform, and temporarily clamp it in place. Now, turn this assembly over, and drive the screws through the holes you just drilled to attach the box to the platform.

4. Rip and crosscut 14—¼×¾×5¾" trim strips. Miter-cut both ends on 12 of the strips at 15° in the same direction, sawing them to 5⅛" final length. Glue and nail them to the outside of the box where shown on the Exploded View drawing. Now, square your miter gauge and cut the two remaining trim strips 5" long, and then glue and nail them in the center of both box ends.

5. Cut four 1¾" lengths of ³⁄₁₆" dowel for the axle pins. Sand a slight taper on one end of each for easy insertion in the axle holes.

6. Paint or finish your flower wagon. (We painted ours a flat white, and trimmed it with a blue-gray pinstripe.) After the finish dries, mount the wheels, and then insert the ³⁄₁₆" dowel pins through the axle holes.

7. To assemble, place the wheels over the axle dowels. Insert the ³⁄₁₆" dowels through the holes in the ends of the axle dowels to lock the wheels in place.

Project Tool List
Tablesaw
Bandsaw
Scrollsaw
Drill press
   Bits: ³⁄₃₂", ⁹⁄₆₄", ³⁄₁₆", ⁷⁄₁₆", ½", ¾"
   Sanding drum, 2"
Router
   ¼" round-over bit

Note: We built the project using the tools listed. You may be able to substitute other tools or equipment for listed items you don't have. Additional common hand tools and clamps may be required to complete the project.

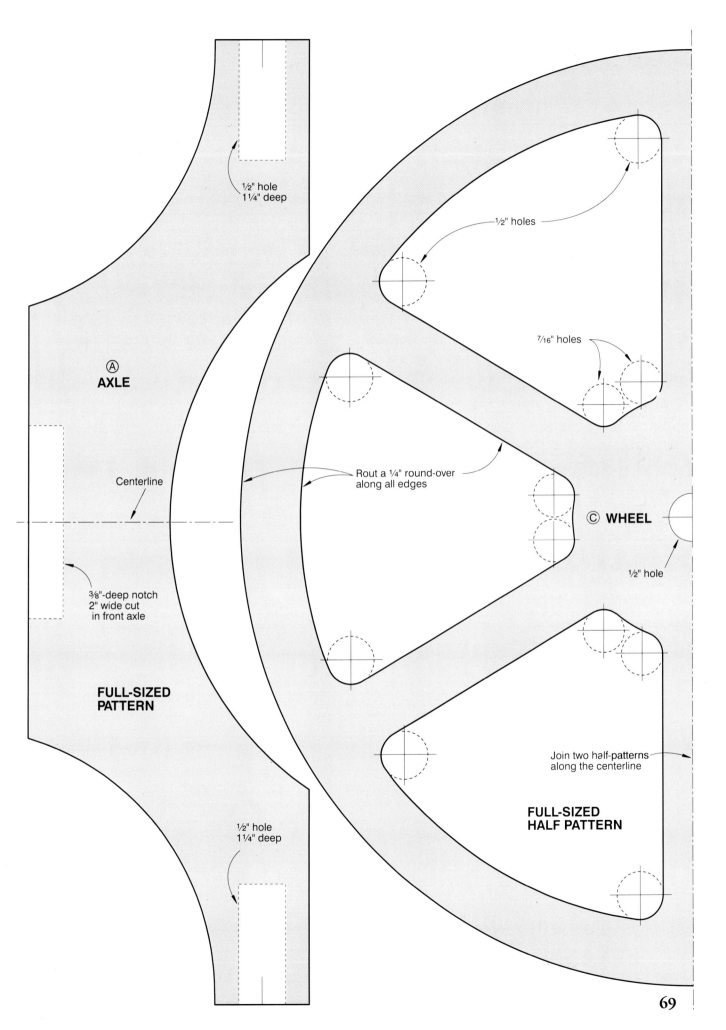

Ⓐ **AXLE**

½" hole
1¼" deep

Centerline

³⁄₈"-deep notch
2" wide cut
in front axle

**FULL-SIZED
PATTERN**

½" hole
1¼" deep

½" holes

⁷⁄₁₆" holes

Rout a ¼" round-over
along all edges

Ⓒ **WHEEL**

½" hole

Join two half-patterns
along the centerline

**FULL-SIZED
HALF PATTERN**

PUTTING FOR PAR WHIRLIGIG

As long as there's a breeze, our whirligig golfer will keep trying to sink his putt.

This golf outing begins by making the base

1. Rip and crosscut a ¾"-thick piece of pine to 2×20⅜". From it, crosscut a 2" length for the stand block (A). Use the remaining piece for the base (B).

2. For the shaft block (C), rip and crosscut a 1½×1½×2" block from a piece of scrap 2×4. Or, you can glue together two pieces of ¾"-thick stock and then trim it to make a same-sized shaft block.

3. Drill and countersink the four ⁹⁄₆₄" shank holes into the base where shown on the Exploded View drawing *opposite,* and the Section View on *page 75.* Drill six ¼" holes

⁷⁄₁₆" deep into the top face of the base for the tabs on the golfers and scenery where shown. Next, draw diagonal lines on the front face of the shaft block to locate the centerpoint. Using your drill press, bore a ⁵⁄₁₆" hole through the block center. Now, bore a ⁵⁄₁₆" hole 1½" deep into the bottom edge of the stand block.

continued

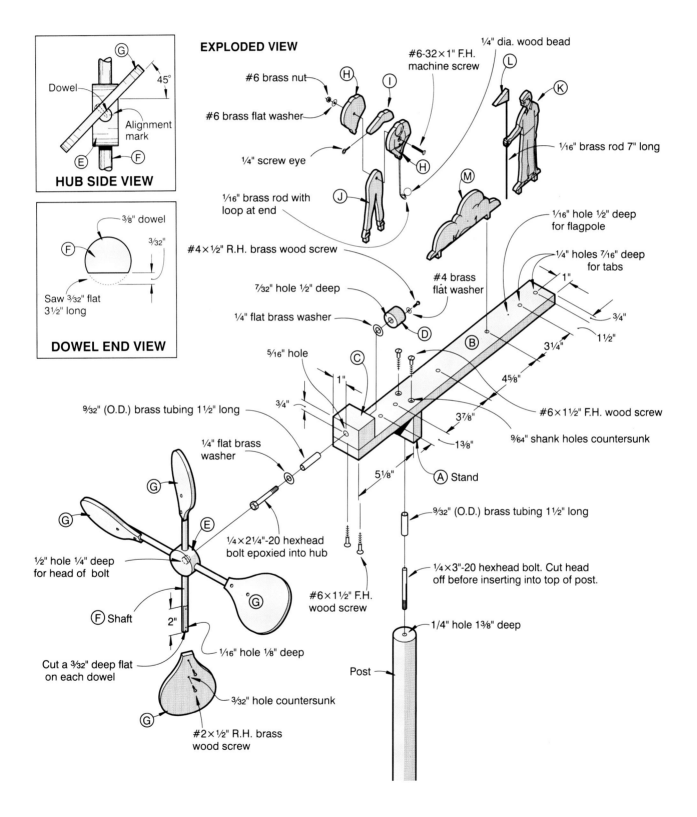

HUB SIDE VIEW

G
Dowel
45°
Alignment mark
E
F

DOWEL END VIEW

⅜" dowel
F
3/32"
Saw 3/32" flat
3½" long

EXPLODED VIEW

#6 brass nut
#6 brass flat washer
¼" screw eye

H
I

#6-32×1" F.H. machine screw

¼" dia. wood bead
L
K

1/16" brass rod with loop at end

H

1/16" brass rod 7" long

#4×½" R.H. brass wood screw

J

7/32" hole ½" deep
¼" flat brass washer

#4 brass flat washer

M

1/16" hole ½" deep for flagpole

¼" holes 7/16" deep for tabs

1"

¾"

1½"

D

B

3¼"

4⅝"

#6×1½" F.H. wood screw

9/64" shank holes countersunk

5/16" hole

C

1"

¾"

3⅞"

1⅜"

A Stand

5⅛"

9/32" (O.D.) brass tubing 1½" long

¼" flat brass washer

G

G

E

¼×2¼"-20 hexhead bolt epoxied into hub

9/32" (O.D.) brass tubing 1½" long

½" hole ¼" deep for head of bolt

F Shaft

2"

G

#6×1½" F.H. wood screw

¼×3"-20 hexhead bolt. Cut head off before inserting into top of post.

1/4" hole 1⅜" deep

Cut a 3/32" deep flat on each dowel

1/16" hole ⅛" deep

3/32" hole countersunk

Post

G

#2×½" R.H. brass wood screw

PUTTING FOR PAR WHIRLIGIG
continued

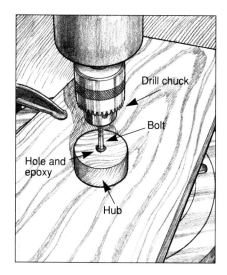

Drill chuck

Bolt

Hole and epoxy

Hub

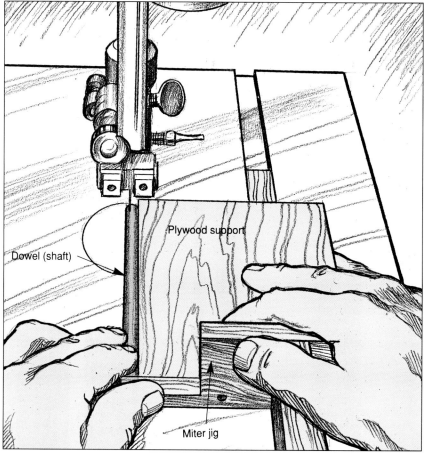

Plywood support

Dowel (shaft)

Miter jig

4. Cut two 1½" lengths of %₂"-outside-diameter brass tubing. (We purchased our tubing at a hobby store, selecting a size that fit over a ¼ x2¼"—20 hexhead bolt.) Insert one of the tubes into the ⁵⁄₁₆" hole in the stand. Insert the second into the hole you drilled through the shaft block.

5. Glue and screw the stand block to the bottom side of the base. (We used Franklin's Titebond II waterproof glue and #6x1½" flathead wood screws to assemble our whirligig.) Attach the shaft block to the top of the base the same way.

Let's make the rotor and propeller
1. Cut a ¾" length of 1¼" dowel for the rotor (D). Or, make a 1¼"-diameter disc from a ¾"-thick piece of scrap maple.

2. Using the dimensions on the Rotor detail on *page 74,* locate and drill the ⁷⁄₃₂" center hole ½" deep. Next, locate and drill the ¹⁄₁₆" hole ⅜" deep on the opposite face. Add a #4 flat brass washer and a #4x½" roundhead brass wood screw.

3. For the propeller hub (E), rip and crosscut a ¾"-thick piece of scrap maple to 1¾" square. To find the center, draw diagonal lines on

one face. See the Hub detail on *page 74.* With a combination square, divide the hub into four equal sections. Extend these lines onto the four edges, and mark the centerpoints on each edge. Scribe a ⅞"-radius (1¾"-diameter) circle on the square's face.

4. Clamp the maple square on edge in a handscrew clamp as shown *above left,* and drill a ⅜" hole ½" deep into the edge's centerpoint. Next drill identical holes in the other three edges. Bore the ½" center hole ¼" deep. Now, bandsaw or scrollsaw the hub to shape. (We sawed just outside the line, and then sanded to the line.) Epoxy the head of a ¼ x2¼" hexhead bolt in the center hole. (As shown *above left,* we chucked the end of the bolt

in our drill press to hold it square in the hub while the epoxy set up.)

5. For the propeller shafts (F), crosscut four 4½" lengths of ⅜" dowel. Scribe a mark 2" from one end on each. Now, using a miter jig and a piece of plywood as shown *above,* bandsaw the ³⁄₃₂" flat surface on one side of each dowel, cutting to the 2" mark. See the Dowel End View drawing on *page 71* for more details.

6. For the propeller blades (G), cut four 4x4½" blanks from ¼"-thick hobby or exterior plywood. (We purchased the plywood at a hobby store.) Stack the blanks face-to-face, using double-faced tape.

7. Using a photocopier or carbon paper, make copies of the patterns (G, H, I, J, K, L, M) *opposite.*

continued

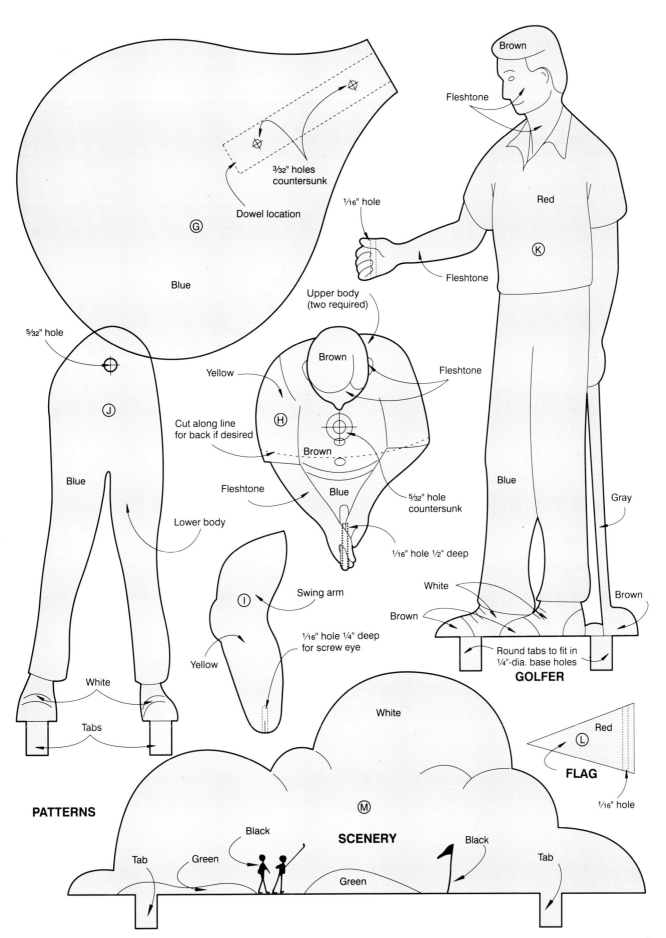

3⁄32" holes countersunk

Dowel location

G

Blue

Upper body (two required)

1⁄16" hole

Brown

Fleshtone

Red

K

Fleshtone

5⁄32" hole

Yellow

Brown

J

Fleshtone

H

Brown

Cut along line for back if desired

Fleshtone

Blue

5⁄32" hole countersunk

Blue

Blue

Lower body

1⁄16" hole 1⁄2" deep

Gray

Swing arm

I

White

Yellow

1⁄16" hole 1⁄4" deep for screw eye

Brown

White

Round tabs to fit in 1⁄4"-dia. base holes

Brown

GOLFER

Tabs

White

White

PATTERNS

M

Red

L

FLAG

1⁄16" hole

Black

Green

SCENERY

Black

Tab

Green

Tab

PUTTING FOR PAR WHIRLIGIG
continued

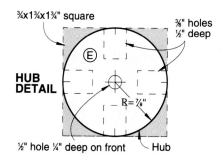

¾x1¾x1¾" square

⅜" holes
½" deep

**HUB
DETAIL**

Ⓔ

R=⅞"

½" hole ¼" deep on front — Hub

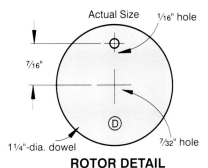

Actual Size

1/16" hole

7/16"

Ⓓ

1¼"-dia. dowel

7/32" hole

ROTOR DETAIL

Include the figure details and painting outlines. Next, trace the blade pattern onto the top blank of the stack, and then bandsaw the blades to shape. Sand the edges, separate the parts, and remove the tape.

8. Center, glue, and clamp a blade to the flat area on each shaft. After the glue cures, drill and countersink two ³⁄₃₂" holes through each blade where shown. Drive a #2x½" flathead brass wood screw into each hole.

9. Secure the whirligig base in a vise or clamp. Insert a prop shaft into each hub hole, and set the blades at a 45° angle as shown on the Hub Side View on *page 71.* Insert the hub bolt through the shaft block, and spin the propeller to test its balance. To adjust its balance, move the shafts in or out of the hub. When it spins smoothly, scribe depth and alignment marks around the base of each shaft, and then number each shaft and mating hole. Now, glue and reassemble the propeller, aligning the parts where previously marked.

Cut out your twosome and the sunny-day scene

1. Transfer the remaining pattern outlines and figure details (we used carbon paper) onto ¼"-thick hobby or exterior plywood. Scrollsaw the figures and scenery to shape.

Note: *The upper body pattern (H) of the putting golfer serves as both the front and back upper body part. If you want the golfer putting on both sides, cut duplicate fronts. If you want him putting on one side only, cut the back (H) piece along the dashed line. Also, you need to sand the lower body (J) to reduce thickness and friction.*

2. Drill and countersink the ⁵⁄₃₂" holes through the body parts where indicated on the patterns. Drill a ¹⁄₁₆" hole ½" deep into the hands for the club shaft. Drill the ¹⁄₁₆" hole in the end of the swing arm and then turn a screw eye into the hole. Now, glue and assemble the putting golfer as shown on the Exploded View drawing. Drill a ¹⁄₁₆" hole vertically through the center of the flag-tender's hand for the flag pole.

3. Round the tabs on the base of the golfers and the scenery to fit into the ¼" base holes. Next, place the flag-tending golfer (K) on the base, insert a ¹⁄₁₆" brass rod through the hole in his hand, and mark the spot where it touches the base. Drill a ¹⁄₁₆" hole ½" deep where marked.

4. To shape the putter, temporarily place the tabs of the putting golfer in the base holes. Cut a 3½" length of ¹⁄₁₆" brass rod, and with a needle-nosed pliers, bend a loop at one end. Now, trim the rod to 3¼" long, and then epoxy the end in the putting golfer's hands. Epoxy a ¼"-diameter wood bead onto the front of the rod loop to serve as a golf ball.

5. Cut a ¾x1" rectangle from ¼" plywood. Trace the flag pattern onto the face of the piece, and drill a ¹⁄₁₆" hole vertically through it where shown for the pole (brass

rod). Now, cut the flag (M) to shape, and then epoxy it onto the tip of the brass rod. Paint your flag red.

It's nearly tee time—just paint and assemble

1. Paint the parts with exterior enamel paints. Apply your choice of colors or follow our paint scheme. (We painted the base green, and the propeller, shaft block, and rotor blue. See the colors printed on the patterns for how we painted the remaining parts.)

2. Assemble the propeller, hub, and putter as shown on the Section View drawing *opposite.* (We applied a coating of white grease to the bolt before inserting it through the brass tube in the shaft block. Note placement of the brass washers. Then, we applied epoxy to the bolt threads and threaded the rotor onto the bolt until there was no shaft end play.) Let the epoxy set up.

3. Glue the golfers and scenery to the base. Cut a 7" length of ¹⁄₁₆" brass rod, insert it through the hand of the flag-tending golfer, and epoxy the end of it in the base hole.

4. From a length of ¹⁄₁₆" brass rod, make the drive rod connecting the rotor and putting golfer. To determine the rod length, center the putter straight up and down. Center the small screw of the rotor at either the 3 or 9 o'clock position. (Our rod measures 3⅜" from loop center to loop center.) Test the whirligig action. Adjust the rod length if necessary for smooth operation.

5. Prepare your whirligig for mounting as shown on the Exploded View drawing. Grease the exposed bolt in the post, and then place the whirligig stand block over it.

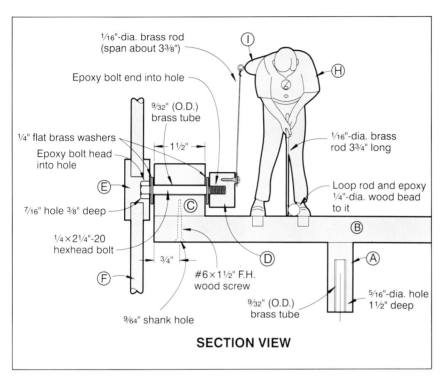

¹/₁₆"-dia. brass rod (span about 3³/₈")

Epoxy bolt end into hole

⁹/₃₂" (O.D.) brass tube

¹/₄" flat brass washers

Epoxy bolt head into hole

Ⓔ

⁷/₁₆" hole ³/₈" deep

¹/₄ × 2¹/₄"-20 hexhead bolt

Ⓕ

1¹/₂"

Ⓒ

3/4"

Ⓓ

#6 × 1¹/₂" F.H. wood screw

⁹/₆₄" shank hole

⁹/₃₂" (O.D.) brass tube

Ⓘ

Ⓗ

¹/₁₆"-dia. brass rod 3³/₄" long

Loop rod and epoxy ¹/₄"-dia. wood bead to it

Ⓑ

Ⓐ

⁵/₁₆"-dia. hole 1¹/₂" deep

SECTION VIEW

Project Tool List
Tablesaw
Bandsaw
Scrollsaw
Drill press
  Bits: ¹/₁₆", ³/₃₂", ⁹/₆₄", ⁵/₃₂", ⁷/₃₂", ¹/₄", ⁵/₁₆", ³/₈", ⁷/₁₆", ¹/₂"
Finishing sander

Note: *We built the project using the tools listed. You may be able to substitute other tools or equipment for listed items you don't have. Additional common hand tools and clamps may be required to complete the project.*

Bill of Materials

Part	Finished Size*			Mat.	Qty.
	T	W	L		
A stand	¾"	2"	2"	P	1
B base	¾"	2"	18½"	P	1
C shaft block	1½"	1½"	2"	P	1
D rotor	1¼" dia.		¾"	D	1
E hub	¾"	1¾" dia.		M	1
F shaft	⅜" dia.		4½"	D	4
G* blade	¼"	4"	4½"	PW	4
H* upper body	¼"	2½"	3"	PW	2
I* swing arm	¼"	1¼"	2½"	PW	1
J* lower body	¼"	2"	5"	PW	1
K* golfer	¼"	4"	7½"	PW	1
L* flag	¼"	1"	1½"	PW	1
M* scenery	¼"	3½"	7"	PW	1

*Cut parts marked with * from ¼" hobby plywood using patterns during construction. Read the instructions before cutting.

Material Key: P–pine; M–maple; PW–¼" hobby or exterior plywood; D–dowel stock
Supplies: 2– ¹/₁₆" brass rods, 1– ⁹/₃₂" O.D. brass tube, ¼X2¼"–20 hexhead bolt, ¼X3"–20 hexhead bolt, 1¼"-dia. dowel, #6X1¼" flathead wood screws, #4X½" flathead brass screws, #4 brass flat washer, 2– ¼" flat brass washers, ¼" screw eye, ⅜" dowel, ¼" wood bead, #6–32X1" flathead machine screw and #6 nut, waterproof glue, epoxy, paints.

STATELY PLANTER

Indoors or out, this traditional planter can perk up any number of appropriate locations around the home—your patio, entry, or screened porch. You may even want a matching pair. Constructed of western cedar, it stands 22" high, and measures 19" across.

Make up the box first

1. For the box sides (A and A1), rip and crosscut eight 6⅜×15½" pieces from ¾"-thick cedar. (See the Cutting Diagram *opposite.*) Glue, edge-join and clamp two pieces together to make a box side. Edge-join the remaining three sides, and let the glued panels dry overnight.

Now, square each side, cutting them to 12¾×15".

Note: For joints that will stand up to the extremes of Mother Nature, use Titebond II water-resistant glue, slow-set epoxy, or resorcinol glue.

2. For the cleats, rip at least 105 linear inches of ¾×¾" cedar stock. From it, crosscut two bottom cleats (B) to 15" long. Attach them to the sides (A) where shown on the Box Assembly drawing *opposite,* and as shown *below,* using #6×1¼" galvanized deck screws.

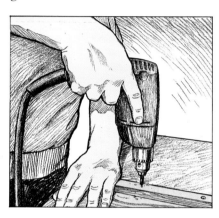

3. Next, crosscut two 13½"-long bottom cleats (C). Center these ¾" from the ends along the *bottom* on the side panels (A1) and attach.

4. To make the bottom (D), rip and crosscut two pieces of ¾" cedar to 7½×15½". Edge-join, and clamp the pieces. Later, remove clamps and trim the panel to 15" square.

5. Using dimensions on the Box Assembly drawing, mark the centerpoints of the ½" drainage holes in the bottom. Drill the holes. (We placed scrap underneath the piece to prevent chip-out when drilling.)

6. Apply glue to the matting edges of the bottom and the cleats on side panels (A). Join these glued pieces and clamp to hold. Drive #6×1¼" deck screws through the bottom to secure it to the cleats as shown *opposite.*

7. From the remaining cleat stock, crosscut four 11¼"-long pieces (E) for the sides. Glue and

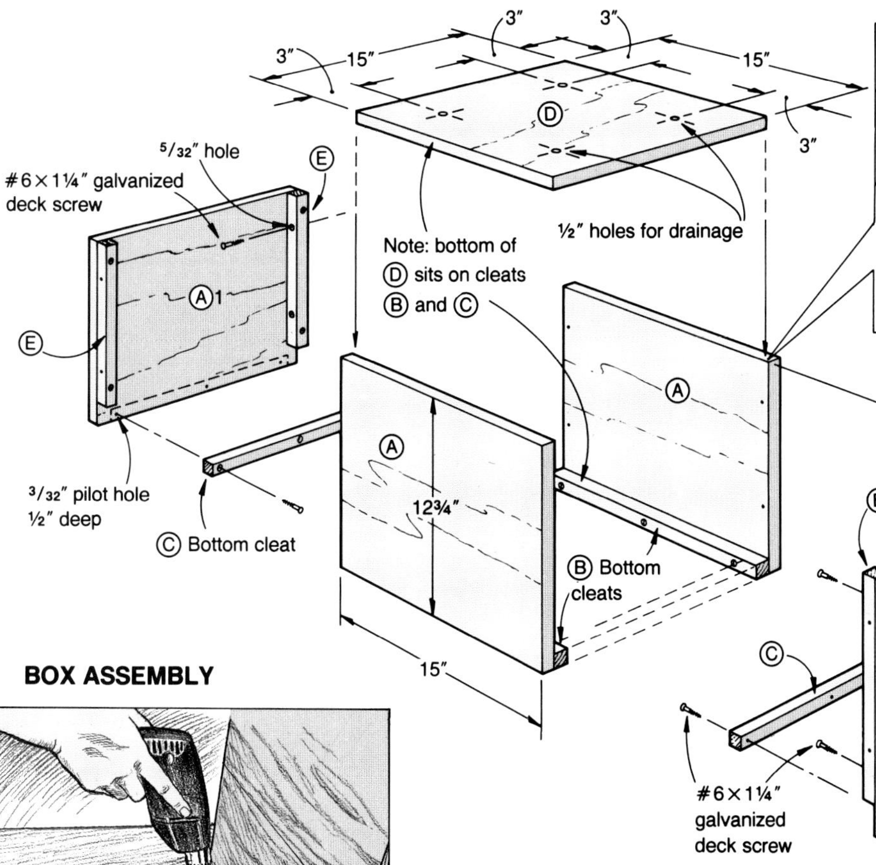
3″
15″
3″
3″
15″
3″
5/32″ hole
#6 × 1¼″ galvanized
deck screw
Ⓔ
Ⓓ
Ⓐ1
Ⓔ
Note: bottom of
Ⓓ sits on cleats
Ⓑ and Ⓒ
½″ holes for drainage
Ⓐ
Ⓐ
12¾″
3/32″ pilot hole
½″ deep
Ⓒ Bottom cleat
Ⓑ Bottom
cleats
15″
Ⓔ
Ⓔ
Ⓒ
Ⓐ1
#6 × 1¼″
galvanized
deck screw

BOX ASSEMBLY

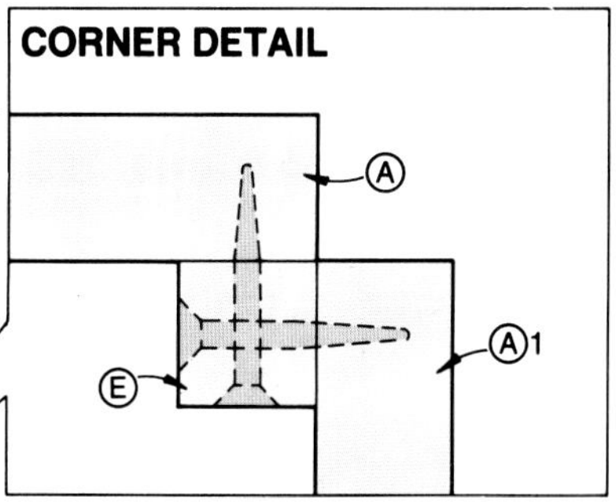
CORNER DETAIL
Ⓐ
Ⓐ1
Ⓔ

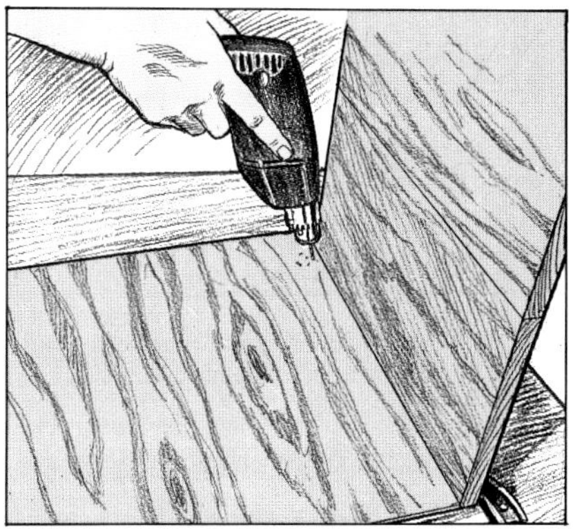

screw them vertically to the A1 side panels where shown on the Box Assembly Drawing. Glue and screw sides A1 to sides A, and to the bottom, driving deck screws through the corner strips and bottom. (See the Box Assembly Drawing and Corner Detail *above* for details.)

Add the legs and caps

1. To make the planter legs (F), crosscut four lengths of 1½ x1½" stock to 21⅝". Angle your tablesaw's blade to 45° from perpendicular, and cut a ⅜" chamfer along all four edges on one end of each piece. Next, measure down ¾" from each chamfered tip, and scribe a line. Now, reset the saw blade to perpendicular, and cut off the

continued

Bill of Materials

Part	Finished Size*			Mat.	Qty.
	T	W	L		
A, A1 sides	¾"	12¾"	15"	C	4
B bottom cleat	¾"	¾"	15"	C	2
C bottom cleat	¾"	¾"	13½"	C	2
D* bottom	¾"	15"	15"	C	1
E vertical cleat	¾"	¾"	11¼"	C	4
F* leg	1½"	1½"	20¾"	C	4
G feet	¾"	2½"	2½"	C	4
H cap	¾"	3"	19"	C	4
I ornament	1½"	1½"	¾"	C	4
J* trim	¼"	¾"	15"	C	4
K* trim	¼"	¾"	9⅜"	C	16
L* trim	¼"	¾"	2½"	C	16
M* trim	¼"	¾"	3"	C	16
N* trim	¼"	¾"	6¼"	C	16

*Parts marked with an * are cut to finished size during construction. Please read all instructions before cutting the material.

Material Key: C–cedar.
Supplies: #6X1¼" galvanized deck screws, #8X2" galvanized deck screws, 4d finish nails, 1"X17 finish brads, 4–⅜" dowel pins, 4–1½"-diameter wood balls, caulk, paint.

CUTTING DIAGRAM

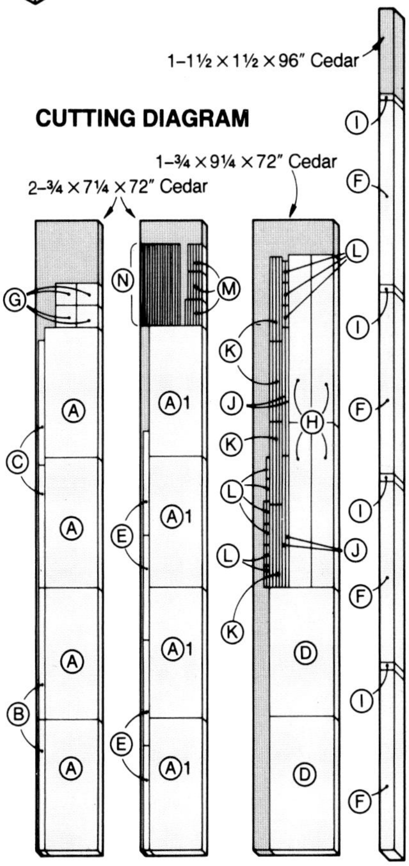
1–1½ × 1½ × 96″ Cedar
1–¾ × 9¼ × 72″ Cedar
2–¾ × 7¼ × 72″ Cedar
Ⓖ
Ⓝ
Ⓜ
Ⓛ
Ⓚ
Ⓙ
Ⓗ
Ⓚ
Ⓛ
Ⓛ
Ⓚ
Ⓙ
Ⓐ
Ⓒ
Ⓐ
Ⓐ
Ⓑ
Ⓐ
Ⓐ1
Ⓔ
Ⓐ1
Ⓐ1
Ⓔ
Ⓐ1
Ⓓ
Ⓓ
Ⓘ
Ⓕ
Ⓘ
Ⓕ
Ⓘ
Ⓕ
Ⓘ
Ⓕ

STATELY PLANTER
continued

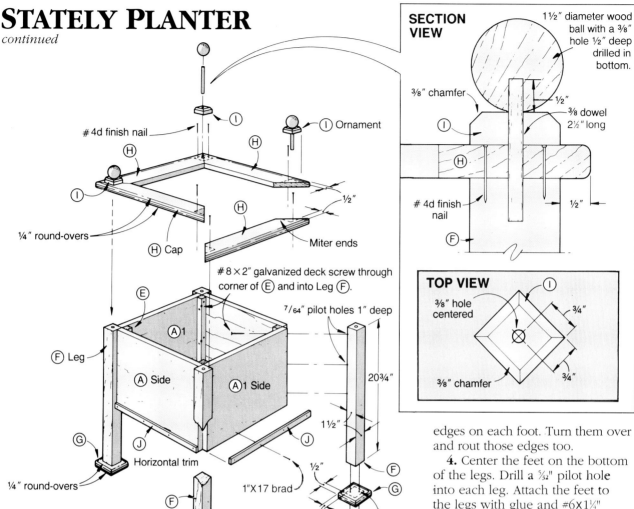

SECTION VIEW

1½″ diameter wood ball with a ⅜″ hole ½″ deep drilled in bottom.

⅜″ chamfer

½″

⅜ dowel 2½″ long

Ⓘ

Ⓗ

4d finish nail

Ⓕ

½″

TOP VIEW

⅜″ hole centered

Ⓘ

¾″

⅜″ chamfer

¾″

4d finish nail

Ⓘ Ornament

Ⓗ

Ⓗ

½″

Ⓗ

¼″ round-overs

Ⓗ Cap

Miter ends

#8 × 2″ galvanized deck screw through corner of Ⓔ and into Leg Ⓕ.

⁷/₆₄″ pilot holes 1″ deep

Ⓔ

Ⓐ1

Ⓕ Leg

Ⓐ Side

Ⓐ1 Side

20¾″

Ⓖ

Ⓙ

Horizontal trim

Ⓙ

1½″

Ⓕ

¼″ round-overs

1″X17 brad

½″

½″

Ⓕ

Ⓖ

⁵/₃₂″ hole

Ⓕ

ⒼFoot

#6x1¼″ galvanized screw

pieces at that line. Save the chamfered pieces you just cut off for use as the leg ornaments (I, L) later.

2. Make sure all four legs measure 20¾″. Trim them if necessary to even length. Next, fit one leg in a corner of the box as shown on the Exploded View drawing *above*. Align the leg flush with the top of the box, and drill and countersink three ⁷/₆₄″ pilot holes through the inside corner cleat (E) and into the leg. Now, attach the leg, gluing and screwing it in place with #8X2″ galvanized deck screws as shown at *right*. Attach the other three corner legs to the planter box the same way.

3. For the feet (G), cut four pieces of ¾″-thick cedar to 2½″ square. Mark centerpoints for the ⁵/₃₂″ holes in

each. Next, drill and countersink the holes on both sides. Temporarily screw the squares to a piece of plywood scrap, and clamp the scrap to your bench. With your router and a ¼″-round-over bit, round over the

edges on each foot. Turn them over and rout those edges too.

4. Center the feet on the bottom of the legs. Drill a ⁵/₃₂″ pilot hole into each leg. Attach the feet to the legs with glue and #6X1¼″ galvanized deck screws.

5. Rip and crosscut two pieces of ¾″ cedar to 3X40″. Clamp one piece to the edge of your workbench and rout a ¼″ round-over along the top and bottom of one edge. Round over the other piece the same way. Now, miter-crosscut (at a 45° angle) four 19″ lengths (measured long point to long point) from it for the box caps (H).

6. Apply glue along one top edge of the box and place a cap piece on it. Allow it to protrude ½″ beyond the legs as shown in the Section View drawing *above*. Mark nail locations, and drive finish nails through the cap and into the leg top. (We drilled ³/₆₄″ pilot holes through the caps for nailing.) Add the other caps the same way. (We attached the opposing caps first, and used bar clamps to snug the other caps into place.)

7. Strike diagonal lines from the corners on the top surface of the chamfered ornament parts (I) you cut to shape in step 1. Glue one at each corner. Using a portable drill, drill a ⅜" hole (see Top View drawing *opposite*) through the ornaments' centerpoints and 2⅝" into the legs.

8. Clamp a piece of scrap to your drill press table. Using a 1¼" spade bit, bore almost through the scrap. Change to a ⅜" twist or Forstner bit. Next, place a 1½"-diameter wood ball in the hole, and drill ½" into it as shown at *right*. Now, drill the remaining three balls.

9. Cut four 2½" lengths of ⅜"-diameter dowel, and sand slight bevels on the ends. Apply glue to the holes drilled in step 7. Tap the dowels into the holes. Glue the balls on the ends of the protruding dowels. (See the Section View drawing *opposite*.)

Apply the trim, and then paint your planter

1. Set up your tablesaw and rip 32 linear feet of ¼x¾" trim stock.

Using the angles and lengths in the Parts View of the Trim Detail drawing *below,* miter-cut enough (16) K pieces for all four sides. Glue and nail them in place (we used 1"x17 brads). Cut the L trim parts and attach them. Do the same for the M parts. Cut four N parts to test-fit. If they don't line up as

shown, adjust length. Cut and install the remaining N parts.

2. Fill all nail holes, and then finish-sand the planter. Apply an exterior-grade oil- or latex-base paint (we used an oil-base paint). Let the paint dry. Now, find a deserving plant to give life to your project.

Project Tool List
Tablesaw
Portable drill
Drill press
   Bits: ³⁄₃₂", ⁷⁄₆₄", ⁵⁄₃₂", ⅜", ½", 1¼"
Router
   ¼" round-over bit
Finishing sander

Note: *We built the project using the tools listed. You may be able to substitute other tools or equipment for listed items you don't have. Additional common hand tools and clamps may be required to complete the project.*

TRIM DETAIL

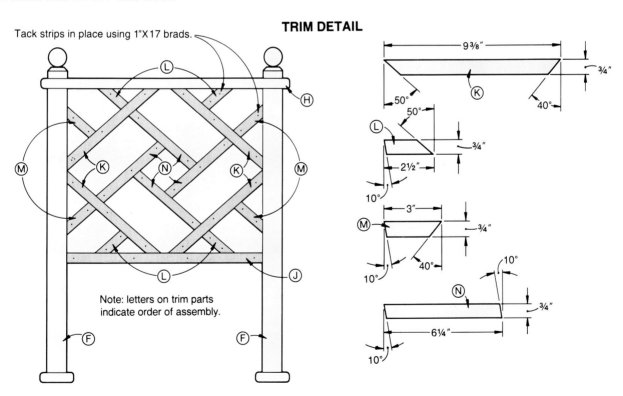

LOW-VOLTAGE LIGHTING

You'll be able to enjoy your beautiful yard and walkways 'round the clock once you build a set of these landscape lighting fixtures. We've kept the construction simple, and because the lights operate at 12 volts, you can wire the system yourself—safely and inexpensively. Best of all, operating these handsome fixtures costs only about 5 cents an evening.

Note: The instructions, Bill of Materials, and Cutting Diagram give the directions and number of pieces needed to build a single light box. To make additional boxes, be sure to cut all identical pieces at the same time to ensure uniformity.

Construct the light boxes to get rollin'

1. Cut the center panel strips (A) to the size listed in the Bill of Materials plus 2" in length. Now, crosscut a 1¼"-long spacer (B) from one end of each center strip. Then, trim each center strip (A) to a 16¾" finished length. And finally, cut the side strips (C, D) to size.

2. With the ends and surfaces flush, glue and clamp each of the two narrow redwood panels (A, B, C) and the two wide panels (A, B, D) together as shown in the photo on the *opposite page.* (Note that we protected the relatively soft redwood from the metal clamp jaws with scrap blocks. We also used resorcinol, a waterproof adhesive, for our light boxes.) Immediately wipe or scrape off excess glue.

3. Rip and crosscut the red-wood shelf cleats (E) to size.

Bill of Materials

Part	Finished Size*			Mat.	Qty.
	T	W	L		
A* center panel	¾"	3½"	16¾"	R	4
B* spacer	¾"	3½"	1¼"	R	4
C side strip	¾"	½"	24"	R	4
D side strip	¾"	1¼"	24"	R	4
E shelf cleats	¾"	¾"	4¼"	R	2
F lamp shelf	¾"	4⅜"	4⅜"	R	1
G* corner cleat	½"	½"	7⅞"	R	4
H lid top	1½"	6"	6"	LR	1
I lid bottom	¾"	4½"	4½"	R	1
J stake	1½"	3½"	32"	R	1

*Cut parts marked with an * larger initially, and trim them to finished size as directed in the how-to instructions.

Material Key: R–redwood, LR–laminated redwood
Supplies: #8X1¼" flathead brass wood screws, 2" galvanized deck screws, stain, finish, ⅛" white acrylic.

4. Mark a hole centerpoint ¾" from both ends of both cleats (see the drawing titled Constructing the Light Box for reference). Drill and countersink ⁵⁄₃₂" shank holes at each mark. Now, mark the cleat location on each narrow panel (A, B, C); see the above-mentioned drawing for positioning particulars. Lightly clamp or tape the cleats in place. Using the previously drilled shank holes as guides, drill a pair of ⁷⁄₆₄" pilot holes ½" deep into each side panel. Secure cleats into position with #8X1¼" wood screws.

5. With the ends and surfaces of the four side panels flush, glue and clamp together. Check for square. Immediately remove excess glue.

6. Sand the light box smooth. Fit your router with a chamfer bit, and rout a ½" chamfer along the inside

Using wood clamp blocks to prevent denting the soft redwood, glue and clamp each lightbox side panel together.

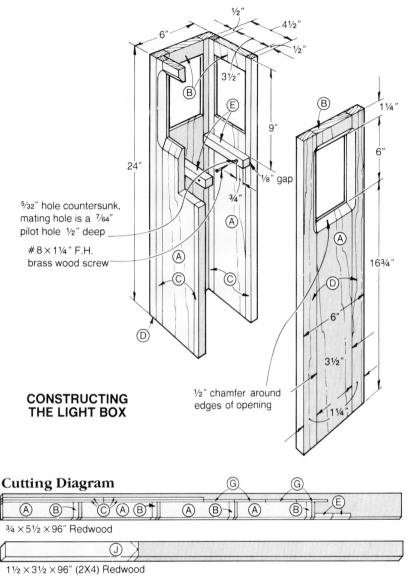

⁵⁄₃₂" hole countersunk, mating hole is a ⁷⁄₆₄" pilot hole ½" deep

#8 × 1¼" F.H. brass wood screw

½" chamfer around edges of opening

⅛" gap

CONSTRUCTING THE LIGHT BOX

Cutting Diagram

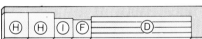

¾ × 5½ × 96" Redwood

1½ × 3½ × 96" (2X4) Redwood

¾ × 7¼ × 48" Redwood

edges of each window opening. To prevent chip-out, rout the chamfer in two passes.

7. Mark the centerpoints, and drill two ⅛" holes in the back panel where dimensioned on the Ground Stake Drawing on *page 83.* You'll later insert screws through these holes when fastening the box to the ground stake.

Lamp shelf and corner cleats come next

1. Cut the lamp shelf (F) to size. Draw diagonal lines (corner to

corner) on the lamp shelf. Drill a 1⅜" hole through the shelf at the marked centerpoint for the bulb socket. (We used a spade bit to drill the hole.) Now, drill a ¾" drain hole in the shelf to prevent water from accidentally becoming trapped inside. Position the shelf on the cleats in the box.

2. To make the four corner cleats (G), start by cutting a piece of redwood to ½X½X32".

3. Now, chuck a straight bit into your table-mounted router. Using
continued

LOW-VOLTAGE LIGHTING
continued

the two-step drawing *below* for reference, rout a pair of ⅛" rabbets ¼" deep the length of the redwood strip. (You also could use a dado blade mounted to your tablesaw to form the rabbets.)

4. Crosscut four corner cleats (G) to length from the 32" rabbeted redwood strip.

5. Glue a redwood cleat in each corner of each light box as shown in the photo *below right*. (We applied glue to the mating edges. Then, with the shelf in place, we held the cleats in position with masking tape.) Immediately remove glue squeeze-out from the rabbets (we used a thin strip of wood to remove the excess glue). After the glue has dried, remove the tape.

6. Using the tablesaw fitted with a carbide-tipped blade, cut the ⅛" white acrylic panels to 3⅞x7⅜". Home centers sell this material for ceiling lights. Check each acrylic panel for proper fit. You want a ¹⁄₁₆" gap between the acrylic and the corner cleats to allow for expansion and contraction of the light box. (We forgot to do this the first time around, and later we had to replace a cracked panel.)

To top it all off, construct the lid
1. From ¾"-thick redwood stock, cut two 6" squares and one 4½" square for the lid pieces (H, I). Glue and clamp the two 6" squares

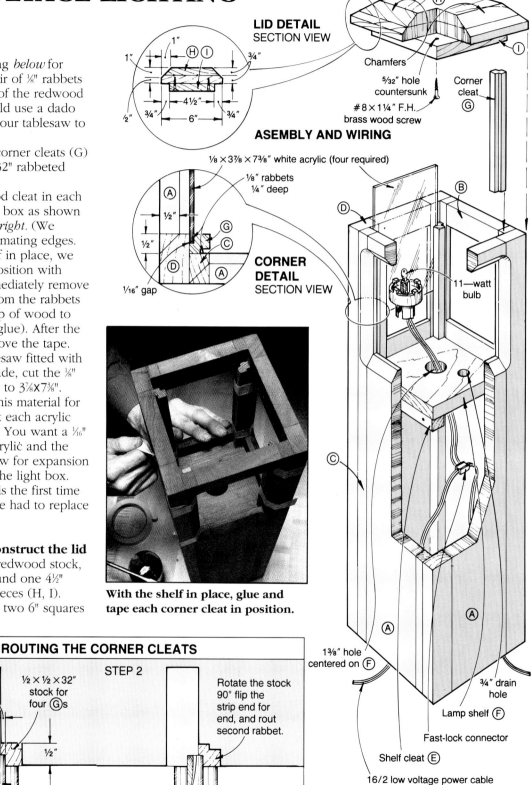

LID DETAIL
SECTION VIEW

Chamfers
⁵⁄₃₂" hole countersunk
#8 × 1¼" F.H. brass wood screw
Corner cleat G

ASEMBLY AND WIRING

⅛ × 3⅞ × 7⅜" white acrylic (four required)
⅛" rabbets ¼" deep

CORNER DETAIL
SECTION VIEW

¹⁄₁₆" gap

11—watt bulb

1⅜" hole centered on F

¾" drain hole

Lamp shelf F
Fast-lock connector
Shelf cleat E
16/2 low voltage power cable

With the shelf in place, glue and tape each corner cleat in position.

ROUTING THE CORNER CLEATS

STEP 1
Router fence
⅛"
¼"
½ × ½ × 32" stock for four Gs
½"
Router table
Straight bit

STEP 2
Rotate the stock 90° flip the strip end for end, and rout second rabbet.

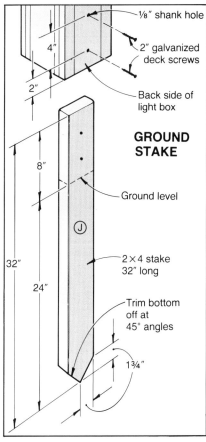

GROUND STAKE

- ¹⁄₈″ shank hole
- 2″ galvanized deck screws
- Back side of light box
- 4″
- 2″
- 8″
- Ground level
- 32″
- 24″
- J
- 2 × 4 stake 32″ long
- Trim bottom off at 45° angles
- 1¾″

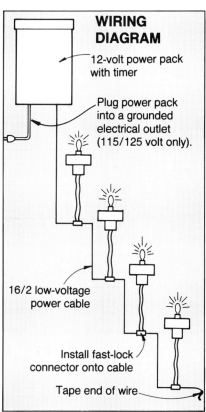

WIRING DIAGRAM

- 12-volt power pack with timer
- Plug power pack into a grounded electrical outlet (115/125 volt only).
- 16/2 low-voltage power cable
- Install fast-lock connector onto cable
- Tape end of wire

together with the edges flush. Allow the glue to dry.

2. Tilt your tablesaw blade 45° from vertical. Using a push block for safety, cut a 1″ chamfer along each edge of the 6″-square lamination.

3. Center and clamp (no glue) the 4½″ square (I) to the bottom face of the chamfered square. Temporarily fasten the squares together with a 1″ brad. Remove the clamp and check the fit of the lid. If the edges of the lid aren't flush with the outside surfaces of the light box, reposition the 4½″ square lid. Drill a pair of pilot holes and screw the 4½″ square in place.

4. Sand the light box and lid. Finish as desired.

Here's how to locate and wire the lights

1. Cut one stake per light box to the size shown on the Ground Stake Drawing at *left*. (We cut ours from a redwood 2x4; a CCA-treated 2x4 would also work.) Trim the bottom of the stake to a point where shown on the drawing.

2. Position the light boxes in your yard where desired.

3. Bare the power cable wires at one end, and connect the bare-wire ends to the power cable terminals on the bottom of the unplugged power pack. Fasten the power pack to a wall within 1′ of a standard grounded electrical outlet (115/125 volt only). Run the power cable from the power pack to the light boxes where shown on the Wiring Diagram drawing. It is not necessary to bury the cable. If you wish to hide the cable from view, bury it a few inches.

4. Push a socket into the 1⅜″ hole in each light box shelf. Run the power cable from the power pack to each light box. Slide each fast-lock connector onto the power cable where a light will be located. (The fast-lock connector pierces the power cable to make the connection; no soldering or wire stripping needed.)

5. Drive a stake into the ground and screw the back of the light box to the stake. Check the box for plumb and tilt accordingly.

6. Slide the acrylic panels into place, add the bulb, and fit a lid onto each light box. Finally, set the timer, settle into a lawn chair, and wait for sundown to enjoy.

At the time of this writing, eight lights are the maximum number you can use with one power pack. We purchased a 12-volt power pack (transformer) with timer, 50 ft. of low-voltage 16/2 cable with eight socket assemblies and eight 11-watt bulbs. This is a common–sized kit sold at most homecenters. Our kit also included a decorative plastic cover for each light assembly. We removed and discarded the plastic covers to make room for the socket and bulb in our wood surrounds.

Project Tool List
Tablesaw
Drill press
    Bits: ⁷⁄₆₄″, ⅛″, ⁵⁄₃₂″, ¾″, 1⅜″
Router
    Router table
    Bits: ⅜″ straight, chamfer
Finishing sander

Note: *We built the project using the tools listed. You may be able to substitute other tools or equipment for listed items you don't have. Additional common hand tools and clamps may be required to complete the project.*

PLANTER/BENCH COMBO

Too often, store-bought patio furniture offers a dull commonplace look; we buy it because there's nothing else around—that is, until now! With our original redwood planter/bench combo, you can add excitement to a drab walk, patio, or deck, especially when the plants reach full bloom. As described here, we built the planters first, and then attached the bench. A shelf inside each of the planters provides a floor for potted plants.

Cut the planter parts

1. Rip and crosscut 12 pieces of 1½"-thick stock (we used construction-grade redwood) to 4½x13⅜" for the frame pieces (A). Crosscut 30° miters on the ends of the pieces where shown on the Frames drawing *opposite, top right.*

2. Rip and crosscut four pieces of 1½"-thick stock to 2¼x26¾" to make the parts labeled B.

3. Dry assemble one frame (three A pieces and one B) on a flat surface. Make certain the miters fit, and mark the pieces so you can return them to their original position. Mark the locations of the dowel pins on adjoining pieces. Using a doweling jig, drill the ⅜" holes into A and B as shown *above right.*

4. Apply a small amount of glue to eight dowel pins and in the holes you drilled in parts A and B. Insert the dowel pins in the holes, assemble the pieces, and clamp as shown *opposite, left,* until the glue dries. (We used a web clamp and Titebond II waterproof glue.)

5. Following the procedures in the previous step, glue, assemble, and clamp the other three frames.

6. After the glue dries, remove the clamps. Next, draw a 9" radius and an 11¼" radius on the face of each frame where indicated by the dotted lines on the Top and Bottom Frame drawing. If you don't have a large compass, make one from a piece of ¼x¾x13" wood. Drill a ⅟₁₆" hole ½" from one end. From it, measure 9" and 11¼" and drill a ⅛" hole at these two points. Place a brad in the small hole and center it on the centerpoint. Place a pencil through the ⅛" holes and scribe the radii as shown *opposite, center.*

7. To make the shelves, rip and crosscut 10 pieces (C) of redwood 2x4 to 3x24". Assemble the pieces into two groups of five as shown on the Shelf drawing *opposite.* Apply glue to the adjoining edges, assemble, and clamp. (We used bar clamps.) After the glue dries, remove the clamps, and sand.

8. Next, using the dimensions on the Shelf drawing, mark the centerpoint for the 11¼" radius on both laminations. Scribe the radii. Drill the ½" drain holes. Saw the frames and shelves to shape with a hand jigsaw.

9. To make the support cleats (D), rip two pieces of redwood stock to 1½" square, and then crosscut them to 22½" long.

10. Make the two planter caps by ripping and crosscutting 6 pieces (E) of ¾"-thick redwood to 5x14¼". Miter-cut both ends of each piece to 30°. Next, rip and crosscut two pieces (F) of ¾" redwood to 3x28½". Assemble the caps as shown on the Planter Cap drawing *opposite.*

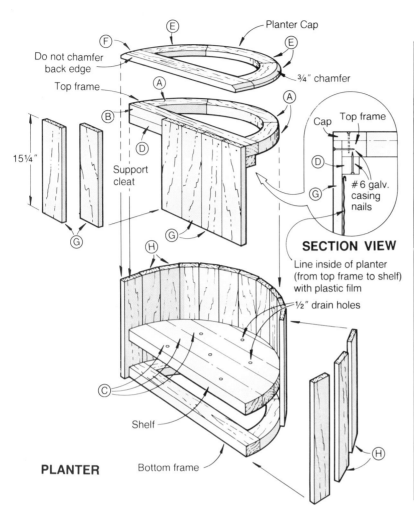

PLANTER

- E
- F — Planter Cap
- E
- Do not chamfer back edge
- A — ¾" chamfer
- Top frame
- B
- A
- D — Cap / Top frame
- 15¼"
- Support cleat

SECTION VIEW

Cap / Top frame
D
G
#6 galv. casing nails

Line inside of planter (from top frame to shelf) with plastic film

½" drain holes

G
H
C
Shelf
Bottom frame
H

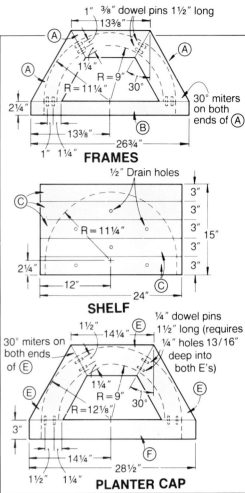

FRAMES

- 1" ⅜" dowel pins 1½" long
- 13⅜"
- A   A
- A
- 1¼"   R = 9"   30°
- R = 11¼"
- 2¼"
- 30° miters on both ends of A
- B
- 13⅜"
- 26¾"
- 1" 1¼"

SHELF

- ½" Drain holes
- C
- R = 11¼"
- C
- 3" 3" 3" 15" 3" 3"
- 2¼"
- 12"
- 24"

PLANTER CAP

- ¼" dowel pins 1½" long (requires ¼" holes 13/16" deep into both E's)
- 1½" 14¼"   E
- 30° miters on both ends of E
- E
- 1¼"   R = 9"   30°
- R = 12⅛"
- E   E
- 3"
- F
- 14¼"
- 28½"
- 1½" 1¼"

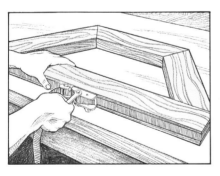

To cut them to shape, use the dimensions on that drawing, and the same procedures you used to make the top and bottom frames in steps 3 and 4. Take your time cutting and sanding the radii on the caps because these edges show. (We cut just outside the lines, and then sanded to the line.)

11. From ¾" stock, rip and crosscut 12 slats (G) and 28 slats (H) to the sizes listed on the Bill of Materials. Rip a 1×2" scrap piece 15¼" long to use as a support.

Next, assemble the planters

1. Turn the top frames upside down. Align one D along the outside edge and both ends of each B as shown on the Planter drawing *above*. Nail it in place.

2. Lay one planter top frame upside down on your bench ¾" in from the edge and clamp it in place. Align a vertical slat (G) at one corner and along the back edge of the top frame. Square the slat to the frame, and drill two ¹⁄₁₆"

pilot holes through the slat, and 1" into B. Apply glue to the slat where it contacts B and D, and then nail the slat to the frame with #6 galvanized casing nails. Attach the remaining five slats the same way.

3. Take the 1×2 scrap piece cut earlier and nail one end of it to the outside edge of the top frame at the center of the half circle. Now, remove the clamps and turn the partially assembled planter right side up, letting the scrap piece temporarily support the curved portion of the top frame. Next, lay the bottom frame on the workbench and clamp it. Place the partially assembled planter on the bottom frame and temporarily nail the bottom end of the 1×2 scrap to the center of the curved outside edge of the bottom frame. Now, attach the free ends of the vertical slats to the bottom frame as shown on the *top of page 86*.

continued

PLANTER/BENCH COMBO

continued

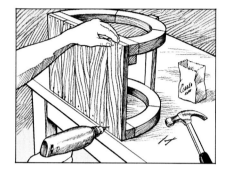

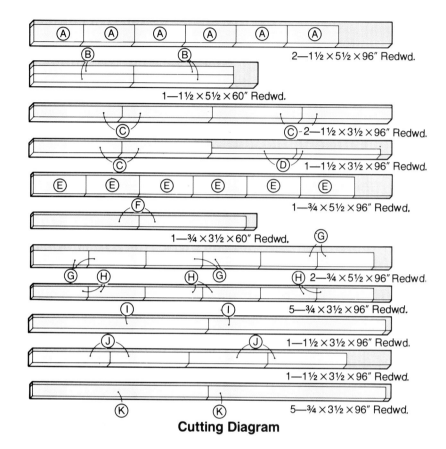

Cutting Diagram

Labels on cutting diagram:
- 2—1½ × 5½ × 96″ Redwd.
- 1—1½ × 5½ × 60″ Redwd.
- C-2—1½ × 3½ × 96″ Redwd.
- 1—1½ × 3½ × 96″ Redwd.
- 1—¾ × 5½ × 96″ Redwd.
- 1—¾ × 3½ × 60″ Redwd.
- 2—¾ × 5½ × 96″ Redwd.
- 5—¾ × 3½ × 96″ Redwd.
- 1—1½ × 3½ × 96″ Redwd.
- 1—1½ × 3½ × 96″ Redwd.
- 5—¾ × 3½ × 96″ Redwd.

4. Determine the height for the shelf and mark its position on parts G and the 1×2 support. (In our planters, we placed the shelves 8″ from the top. If you prefer to fill the planter with soil, you may choose another shelf level. For soil we recommend lining the planter with plastic film and stapling it in place.) Next, tighten wood-screw clamps on the outside G parts and 1½″ below your shelf level marks. Add a third clamp at the same location on the 1×2 brace. Now, rest the shelf on the clamps, and drive a nail through the scrap and into the shelf. Nail the shelf to the slats. Remove the clamps when done.

5. Starting at one side, begin attaching the vertical slats (H) around the planter. When you reach the 1×2 support, remove it. Continue attaching the slats until you have four left. Check their fit in the remaining space. If you need to narrow up the pieces, sand or plane a small amount off the edges of all four pieces rather than from just one. Attach the remaining slats.

6. Position the cap on top of the assembly. Align the straight edges of pieces B and F, and nail the cap to the top frame as detailed in the Section View on the Planter drawing on *page 85.*

7. Assemble the second planter following the same procedures.

Now, make the bench

1. Rip and crosscut two redwood 2×4s to 3×47¼″ for the bench-beams (I), and four to 3×21″ for the cross beams (J). Using the

dimensions on the Exploded View drawing *opposite,* rabbet both bench beams as shown *above.*

2. Rip and crosscut 10 pieces of ¾″ redwood to 2¹⁵⁄₁₆×47¼ for the bench slats (K).

3. Lay out the bench frame on a flat surface. Apply glue to the ends of the four cross beams, and nail the parts together. Glue and nail a slat to each side of the frame.

4. To nail the slats to the top of the bench frame, first mark the center on top of both end cross supports. Next, place a mark ⁄₁₆″ to the side of the centerpoint at both

ends. Align the edge of the first slat with these marks, flush the ends with the frame, and nail it in place. Cut two ⅛″-thick spacers from scrap hardboard or plywood. Now, nail the remaining slats to the frame, using the spacers as shown *above.*

5. To complete the assembly, turn the planters and bench upside down. Align the bench between the two planters, and then place a web clamp around the entire unit to temporarily hold it together. (We combined two web clamps in order to reach all the way around it.)

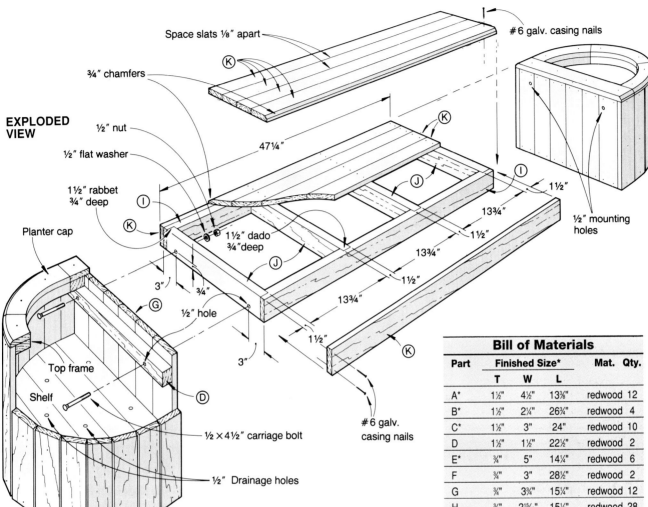

EXPLODED VIEW

Space slats ⅛″ apart

¾″ chamfers

K

#6 galv. casing nails

½″ nut

½″ flat washer

1½″ rabbet ¾″ deep

Planter cap

I

K

47¼″

K

J

J

1½″

13¾″

1½″

½″ mounting holes

13¾″

1½″

I

Top frame

Shelf

3″

¾″

½″ hole

1½″ dado ¾″ deep

13¾″

1½″

G

D

3″

½ × 4½″ carriage bolt

½″ Drainage holes

K

#6 galv. casing nails

Using the dimensions on the Exploded View drawing, locate and drill the ½″ bolt holes through parts D, G, and J where shown. Insert the carriage bolts, and carefully turn the assembly over. Next, reverse the bolts, attach the washers and nuts, and then tighten the nuts. Remove the web clamps.

6. Rout a ¾″ chamfer along the entire top edge on the planters and bench.

7. Set all nails, and fill the nail holes. Finish if desired. We applied two coats of clear wood finish to protect the wood from excessive weathering. Left unfinished, redwood weathers gray.

Project Tool List
Tablesaw
    Dado blade or dado set
Jigsaw
Portable drill
Drill press
    Bits: ¹⁄₁₆″, ⅛″, ¼″, ⅜″, ½″
Router
    Chamfer bit
Belt sander
Finishing sander

Note: *We built the project using the tools listed. You may be able to substitute other tools or equipment for listed items you don't have. Additional common hand tools and clamps may be required to complete the project.*

	Bill of Materials				
Part	**Finished Size***			**Mat.**	**Qty.**
	T	**W**	**L**		
A*	1½″	4½″	13⅜″	redwood	12
B*	1½″	2¼″	26¾″	redwood	4
C*	1½″	3″	24″	redwood	10
D	1½″	1½″	22½″	redwood	2
E*	¾″	5″	14¼″	redwood	6
F	¾″	3″	28½″	redwood	2
G	¾″	3¾″	15¼″	redwood	12
H	¾″	2¹⁵⁄₁₆″	15¼″	redwood	28
I	1½″	3″	47¼″	redwood	2
J	1½″	3″	21″	redwood	4
K	¾″	2¹⁵⁄₁₆″	47¼″	redwood	10

* Parts marked with an * are cut to final size during construction. Please read all instructions before cutting.

Supplies: #6 galvanized casing nails, 32– ⅜×1½″ dowel pins, 16– ¼×1½″ dowel pins, 4– ½×4½″ carriage bolts, 4– ½″ flat washers, 4– ½″ nuts, plastic lining (optional), finish, nail caulk or putty.

PARTY-TIME CART

This hand roll-around cart with its large work surface is perfect for entertaining friends or at family get-togethers. Constructed of weather-resistant white oak, our cart folds up for space-saving storage at the end of the cookout or when the leaves begin to fall.

Note: Because of space limitations, we can't provide full-sized patterns for this project. However, to enable you to build the project, we've included gridded patterns. To enlarge these patterns, see the instructions on page 96.

Let's begin with the legs

1. With scissors, cut the full-sized leg (A, B) patterns to shape. Apply spray adhesive to the back side of the patterns, and then adhere them side by side to the face of a piece of ¾"-thick stock at least 9" wide and 4' long. (We chose white oak because it stands up well to the weather.) Now, using double-faced tape, adhere a second ¾×9×48" board to the underside of the patterned board, aligning the boards along the edges.

2. Bore 1" holes through both boards where marked on the patterns (we used a Forstner bit). Then, bandsaw the taped-together legs (A,B) to shape. (We cut just outside the marked line, and then sanded to the line with our stationary disc and drum sanders.)

3. Separate the four legs and remove the tape and patterns. (We wiped off adhesive residue with lacquer thinner.) Finish-sand the legs, going from 100-grit, to 150-grit, and then finishing with 220-grit sandpaper.

Now, cut the tray parts

1. Rip and crosscut two pieces of ¾"-thick stock to 2½×31¾" for the tray supports (C). Stack the pieces together face-to-face with double-faced tape between them. Now, using the dimensions on the Tray Support drawing *opposite,* lay out the top board by plotting the centerpoints for the holes, the slot, and the two end radii.

2. Bore the 1" and 1⅛" holes through both pieces where marked. Next, bandsaw and sand the tray supports (C) to shape, using the same technique described for preparing the legs. Separate the parts and remove the tape and patterns from the parts. Finish-sand.

3. For the slats (D), start with a piece of stock ½×7¼×74". (We resawed ¾"-thick stock to ½".) Crosscut four 18"-long pieces from the 74"-long piece. Finish-sand both faces of each piece. Now, rip 21 1"-wide slats (D) from the 18"-long pieces. Finish-sand the edges.

4. With a ⅜" countersink/counterbore bit, drill a screw hole centered on and 1⅛" from each end of the tray slats where shown on the Screw Hole detail accompanying the Exploded View drawing on *page 90.* (To simplify the task, we clamped a fence to our drill-press table to center the slats, and used a stopblock to set a uniform hole distance from the ends as shown *opposite, top.*)

For a great tray, keep everything square

1. Before assembling the tray, cut two pieces of scrap ¾" plywood to 2x36" and two pieces to 1¾X15". Clamp the 36"-long pieces to the outside of the tray supports and flush with the top edge where shown *below right*.

2. Set the tray supports on a flat surface about 16½" apart and parallel to each other. Now, clamp the two 15"-long spacers between the tray supports where shown.

3. Beginning opposite the notched end (farthest from the handles on the Exploded View drawing), place the first slat flush with the ends of the tray supports. Next, align the ends of the slat flush with the outside edge of the plywood scraps you clamped to the supports.

4. Center a ⁷⁄₆₄" drill bit in each of the previously drilled mounting holes in the slat, and drill ½"-deep pilot holes into the tray support. Drive a #8X¾" flathead wood screw through each of the holes.

5. Cut a ⅜"-thick spacer 18" long. Use it to space the remaining slats as you attach them one by one to the supports. Remove the scrap, and attach the 21st slat.

6. For screw-hole plugs, cross cut 42 ⁵⁄₁₆" lengths of ⅜" oak dowel and glue one in each of the slat holes. (We used yellow woodworker's glue. If you prefer

continued

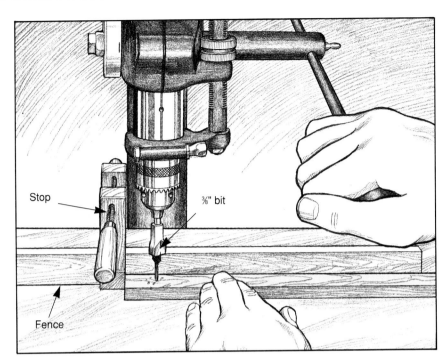

Stop   ⅜" bit

Fence

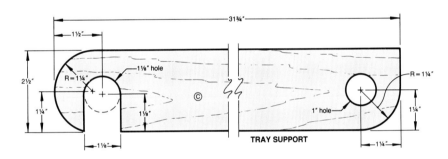

TRAY SUPPORT

Bill of Materials

Part	Finished Size*			Matl.	Qty.
	T	W	L		
A* outside leg	¾"	2½"	46"	O	2
B* inside leg	¾"	2½"	44"	O	2
C tray support	¾"	2½"	31¾"	O	2
D slat	½"	1"	18"	O	21
E* wheel	¾"	10" diam.		EO	2
F collar	½"	2½"	2½"	O	2

* Parts marked with an * are cut to size during construction. Please read all instructions before cutting.

Material Key: O–oak, EO–edge-joined oak
Supplies: spray adhesive, double-faced tape, ⅜" oak dowel plugs, 1" oak dowels, #8X¾" flathead wood screws, ⅜X1" dowel pins, 6d finish nails, finish.

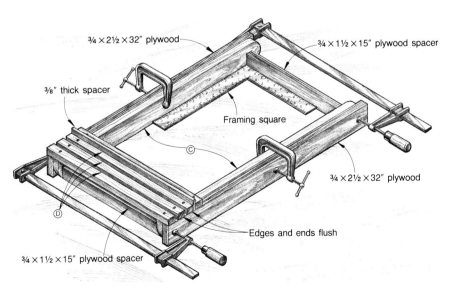

¾ × 2½ × 32″ plywood

¾ × 1½ × 15″ plywood spacer

⅜″ thick spacer

Framing square

¾ × 2½ × 32″ plywood

Edges and ends flush

¾ × 1½ × 15″ plywood spacer

PARTY-TIME CART
continued

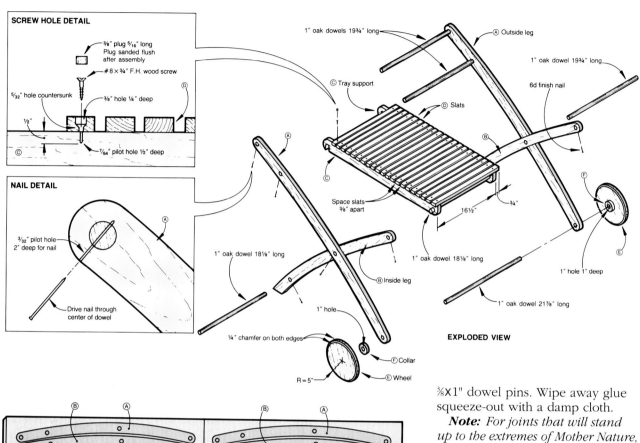

SCREW HOLE DETAIL

⅜" plug ⁵⁄₁₆" long
Plug sanded flush
after assembly

#8 × ¾" F.H. wood screw

⁵⁄₃₂" hole countersunk

⅜" hole ¼" deep

½"

⁷⁄₆₄" pilot hole ½" deep

NAIL DETAIL

³⁄₃₂" pilot hole
2" deep for nail

Drive nail through
center of dowel

1" oak dowels 19¾" long

Ⓒ Tray support

Ⓓ Slats

Ⓐ Outside leg

1" oak dowel 19¾" long

6d finish nail

Ⓑ

Ⓕ

Space slats
⅜" apart

16½"

¾"

1" hole 1" deep

1" oak dowel 18⅛" long

Ⓑ Inside leg

1" hole

Ⓔ

1" oak dowel 21⅞" long

EXPLODED VIEW

¼" chamfer on both edges

Ⓕ Collar

Ⓔ Wheel

R = 5"

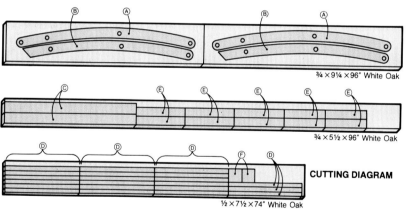

¾ × 9¼ × 96" White Oak

¾ × 5½ × 96" White Oak

½ × 7½ × 74" White Oak

CUTTING DIAGRAM

less-conspicuous face-grain plugs, make them with a plug cutter.) Sand the plugs flush, and then finish-sand the tray.

And now for the wheels

1. From ¾"-thick stock, first rip material to 2⅛" wide. Then, from it, crosscut six pieces to 12" long and four pieces to 10" long for the wheels (E). (To prevent the large-diameter wheels from warping later, we edge-joined the 2⅛"-wide stock.) Joint the cut edges.

2. For each wheel, lay out and dry-clamp (no glue) one 10" piece, three 12" pieces, and another 10" piece in the configuration shown on the Wheel Lamination drawing *opposite*. Mark the mating dowel-hole centerlines on each set where shown on the Wheel Lamination drawing. Remove the clamps.

3. Using a doweling jig, drill ⅜" holes ⁹⁄₁₆" deep into the edges where marked. Glue, assemble, and clamp each lamination with

⅜×1" dowel pins. Wipe away glue squeeze-out with a damp cloth.

Note: *For joints that will stand up to the extremes of Mother Nature, use Titebond II water-resistant glue, slow-set epoxy, or resorcinol glue.*

4. After the glue dries, remove the clamps and scrape the surfaces to remove excess glue. Belt-sand if necessary to flatten the wheel lamination. Then, find the center of each lamination and scribe a 10"-diameter circle. Now, bore a 1" hole ½" deep at the marked centerpoint to receive the axle. Put the most attractive grain on the opposite face of the wheel.

5. Bandsaw the 10"-diameter wheels to shape. Sand to the line with a disc sander. With a ¼" chamfer bit, rout a ¼" chamfer along both edges of each wheel. (If you don't have a table-mounted router, place the lamination on a carpet pad scrap while you chamfer the wheels with a hand-held router.)

6. To make the two wheel collars (F), first adhere two pieces of ½×3×3" stock together with double-faced tape. Use a compass to mark a 2½"-diameter circle on one piece.

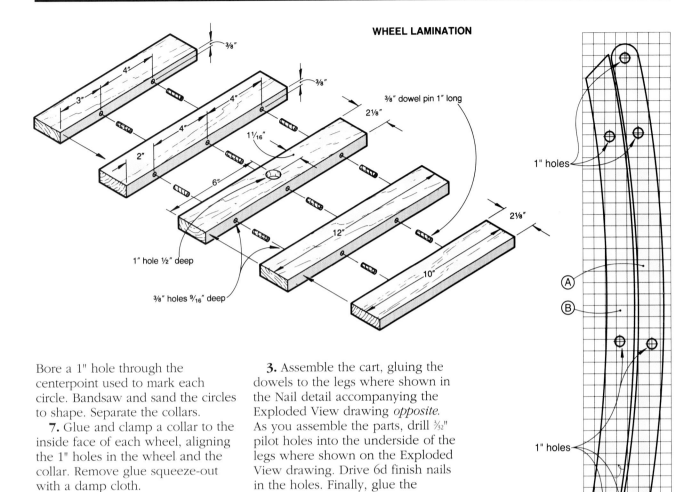

WHEEL LAMINATION

3/8"

4"

3"

3/8"

4"

2"

4"

1 1/16"

3/8" dowel pin 1" long

2 1/8"

6"

1" hole 1/2" deep

3/8" holes 9/16" deep

12"

2 1/8"

10"

1" holes

A

B

1" holes

Each square=1"

GRIDDED LEG PATTERNS

Bore a 1" hole through the centerpoint used to mark each circle. Bandsaw and sand the circles to shape. Separate the collars.

7. Glue and clamp a collar to the inside face of each wheel, aligning the 1" holes in the wheel and the collar. Remove glue squeeze-out with a damp cloth.

Assemble and finish the cart

1. Crosscut four 1" dowels 1/4" longer than specified on the Exploded View drawing *opposite.* Next, dry-fit all of the pieces. Check that the tops of the inside legs have about 1/16" clearance below the slats, that the cart folds without binding, and that the tray sets level when in the open position. Adjust the leg lengths if necessary for a good fit, and to level the cart.

2. Remove the 1" dowels and crosscut them to their final length. Apply the finish of your choice. (We brushed on three coats of an exterior polyurethane, sanding between coats.) To prevent the finish from running onto the surfaces to be glued, we wrapped 3/4"-wide masking tape inside each 1" hole and then wrapped the tape around the dowel axle ends.

3. Assemble the cart, gluing the dowels to the legs where shown in the Nail detail accompanying the Exploded View drawing *opposite.* As you assemble the parts, drill 3/32" pilot holes into the underside of the legs where shown on the Exploded View drawing. Drive 6d finish nails in the holes. Finally, glue the wheels to the 1" axle dowel.

Project Tool List
Tablesaw
Bandsaw
Portable drill
Drill press
   Bits: 3/32", 7/64", 5/32", 3/8", 1", 1 1/8"
Router
   Router table
   Chamfer bit
Belt sander
Finishing sander

Note: We built the project using the tools listed. You may be able to substitute other tools or equipment for listed items you don't have. Additional common hand tools and clamps may be required to complete the project.

NEIGHBORLY NUMBERS

With this project, no one–not even the pizza deliveryman—will have trouble finding your house by day or night. By day, this sign offers a cheery welcome. At night, 4" backlighted numerals won't leave any question as to where you call home.

Cut the parts from cedar

1. From a 24" length of 1⅟₁₆×6" cedar decking stock, rip ½" off one edge, then reset the fence and rip a 3½"-wide strip to square the edges. From this strip, crosscut one 16" length for the sign board (A), two 2¼" lengths for the sides (B), and two 1×1×3½" pieces for the cleats (C). If your house has lap siding, crosscut one end of each side at an angle to offset the siding's slope.

Note: *As pictured, the 16" sign board (A) holds four numerals. If you have more numerals in your street address, buy extra stock and add 4" to the length for each additional numeral (3" if numeral 1). Center WELCOME on the sign board.*

2. Using carbon paper or a photocopier, make a copy of the Welcome patterns, and the numbers on *pages 94–95* that you'll use. Join the two Welcome patterns to complete the word and then cut around the outside, leaving a ¼" margin around the word.

3. Scribe a faint line ⅞" from the bottom on the face of the sign board, and 1¾" in from each end. Next, apply a light misting of spray adhesive to the back of the pattern. Place the pattern on the board, aligning the bottom of the letters on the horizontal line, and centering between the two vertical lines.

4. To recess the Welcome letters in the sign board, first angle the scrollsaw table to 2½° from perpendicular to make a bevel cut. (Cutting on a bevel closes the saw kerf space when you push in the cutout.) Test by cutting a circle on a piece of 1⅟₁₆" scrap, and then push the cutout into the piece to make certain it does not fall out. If it does fall out, tilt the table one more degree, and test again. (We used #5 scrollsaw blades with 12½ teeth per inch.)

5. You need to drill the start holes in the sign board at the same angle you'll be sawing the letters. To do this, place the board face up on your drill-press table. Next, put a ⅛"-thick scrap under the piece, near the top edge, to tilt WELCOME at an angle to the drill bit. Now, drill ⅟₁₆" start holes where shown on each letter. Before drilling the start hole for the *inside* line of the O letter, move the scrap to the bottom edge so it tilts WELCOME in the *opposite* direction.

6. Thread your scrollsaw blade through the first start hole, and then saw around the letter. (We centered the saw blade on the line.) When sawing, keep the letter on the *downhill side* of the blade to maintain the bevel. Cut around the remaining letters—except inside the O—the same way. When cutting out the inside of letter O, keep the letter on the *uphill side* of the blade.

7. Rip and crosscut a 15" length (longer if you need more than four numerals) of the cedar stock to 4½" wide. Adhere the numeral patterns to the face of the piece. (We ran the grain horizontally through the letters to match grain direction on the sign board.) Set your scrollsaw table perpendicular to the blade, and saw out each numeral. Sand the cut edges of the numerals if necessary to smooth the curves.

Begin assembling your sign

1. Place the sign board face up on a flat surface and position ¼"-thick spacers under it at each end. Glue (we used yellow woodworker's glue) each letter (except the O center) in their holes, pushing them through until they touch the surface underneath. After the glue dries, turn the board on its face, and glue the O center in its space, pushing it flush with the front face.

2. After the glue has dried, cut off the excess from the letters on the back side. (We used our tablesaw.) Sand both front and back faces with 100-grit sandpaper. Mark, drill, and counterbore the four holes in the front face of the sign board as detailed on the Exploded View drawing *opposite*. Drill and countersink the holes in each B part and the mounting cleats as dimensioned.

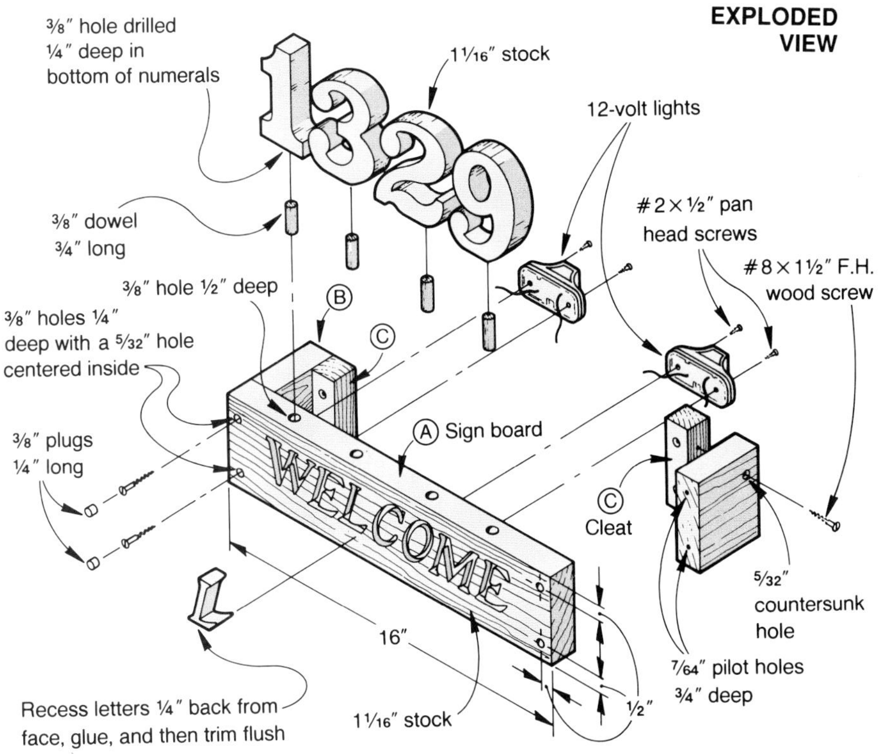
EXPLODED VIEW
3/8″ hole drilled 1/4″ deep in bottom of numerals
1 1/16″ stock
12-volt lights
3/8″ dowel 3/4″ long
#2 × 1/2″ pan head screws
#8 × 1 1/2″ F.H. wood screw
3/8″ hole 1/2″ deep
B
C
3/8″ holes 1/4″ deep with a 5/32″ hole centered inside
3/8″ plugs 1/4″ long
A Sign board
C Cleat
5/32″ countersunk hole
16″
7/64″ pilot holes 3/4″ deep
1/2″
Recess letters 1/4″ back from face, glue, and then trim flush
1 1/16″ stock

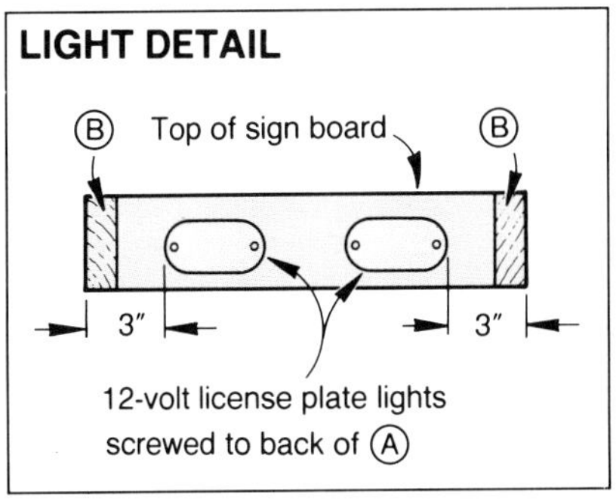
LIGHT DETAIL
B
Top of sign board
B
3″
3″
12-volt license plate lights screwed to back of A

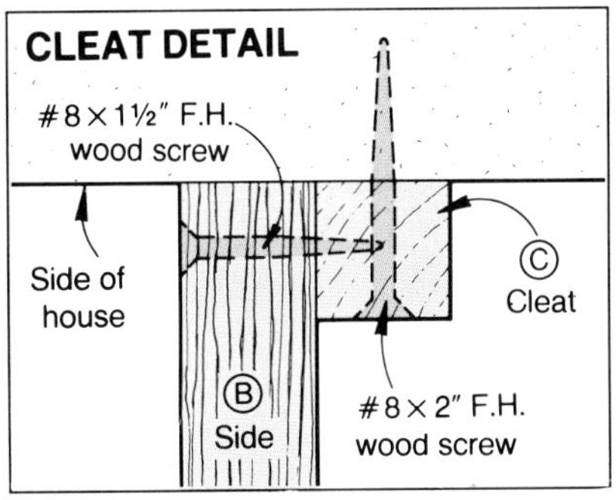
CLEAT DETAIL
#8 × 1 1/2″ F.H. wood screw
Side of house
C
Cleat
B
Side
#8 × 2″ F.H. wood screw

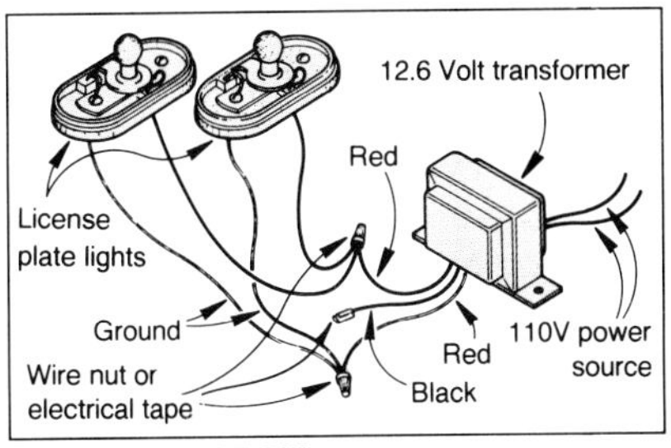
12.6 Volt transformer
Red
License plate lights
Ground
110V power source
Red
Wire nut or electrical tape
Black

WIRING DIAGRAM

3. Arrange your numbers on the top edge of the sign board. Mark a vertical line on the back of the sign board to locate each dowel hole. Using these lines as guides, drill 3/8" holes in the top edge of the sign board. Now, drill matching holes in the bottoms of the letters as instructed on the Exploded View drawing. (We used a doweling jig.)

4. Glue and screw the sides to the back of the sign board. Using a 3/8" plug cutter, make four cedar plugs. Glue them in the counterbored holes in the sign front.

5. Glue 3/4" lengths of 3/8" dowels in the holes in the numerals, and then in the holes in the top of the sign board. Align. After the glue dries, sand the numerals and plugs flush with the sign board's front.

Now, light up the night

1. Mount the lights to the back of the sign board. (We used #2X1/2" panhead screws, and chiseled shallow grooves under the fixture to provide clearance for the wires.) Wire the two lights (we used 18-gauge lamp wire on the low voltage side) as shown on the Wiring diagram at *far right.*

Note: *To backlight the numerals, we attached two 12-volt license plate lights (NAPA part number 425-WD) upside down to the back of the sign board, and wired them through a 12-volt transformer (Radio Shack catalog number 273-1511A). You can wire a switch between the transformer and power supply, or use an existing light switch to control the sign light.*

2. Mount the two cleats to your house as shown on the Cleat detail *above right.* Finally, complete the permanent wiring.

Project Tool List
Tablesaw
Scrollsaw
Drill press
Bits: 1/16", 7/64", 5/32", 3/8"
3/8" plug cutter
Finishing sander

Note: *We built the project using the tools listed. You may be able to substitute other tools or equipment for listed items you don't have. Additional common hand tools and clamps may be required to complete the project.*

continued

Bill of Materials

Part	Finished Size*			Mat.	Qty.
	T	W	L		
A* sign board	1 1/16"	3½"	16"	C	1
B side	1 1/16"	3½"	3½"	C	2
C cleat	1"	1"	3½"	C	2
D numerals	1 1/16"	from pattern as required			

*Length of sign board will vary, depending on the number of numerals required. Read text before cutting any material.

Material Key: C–cedar
Supplies: #8X1½" flathead wood screws, #8X 2" flathead wood screws, #2X½" panhead screws, 12-volt license plate lights (NAPA #425-WD), 12.6-volt transformer (Radio Shack #273-1511A), 18-gauge lamp wire as needed, wire nuts, electrical tape, 3/8" dowel.

Drill ¹⁄₁₆″ start hole

Cut along dashed line for 9

Cut along dashed line for 6

Drill 1/16" start hole

**FULL–SIZED
PATTERNS**

ACKNOWLEDGMENTS

Project Designers

David Ashe—Treat for Tweets Bird Feeder, pages 46–47

Lance Campbell—Humdinger of a Feeder, pages 58–61

James R. Downing—Lazy-Days Porch Swing, pages 5–9; Lazy-Days Porch Rocker, pages 10–15; Adirondack Lawn Chair, pages 16–20; Two-Part Patio Chair, pages 21–25; Mahogany Outdoor Chair, pages 26–31; Mahogany Outdoor Table, pages 32–35; Folding Snack Table, pages 36–37; Fine-Feathered Friend Feeder, pages 43–45; Short Branch Saloon for the Birds, pages 54–55; Stately Planter, pages 76–79; Low-Voltage Lighting, pages 80–83; Planter/Bench Combo, pages 84–87; Party-Time Cart, pages 88–91; Neighborly Numbers, pages 92–95

Kim Downing—Barn Birdhouse, pages 39–42

Marlen Kemmet—Farmers' Seed Company Bird Feeder, pages 48–49

Tom Lewis—Bloomin' Good Wagon, pages 65–69

George Myhervold—Putting for Par Whirligig, pages 70–75

Bob and Carolyn Reichert—Stars-and-Stripes Wren House, pages 56–57

George C. Voss—Flight School Birdhouse, pages 50–53

Photographers

Bob Calmer
John Hetherington
Bill Hopkins
Hopkins Associates
Jim Kascoutas
Hugh P. Smith

Illustrators

Jamie Downing
Kim Downing
Mike Henry
Carson Ode
Ode Designs
Greg Roberts
Jim Stevenson
Bill Zaun

Enlarging gridded patterns by hand

Gridded patterns in this book that require enlargement include the statement "Each square = 1"." This means that no matter what size grid squares you see in the drawing, you *must* enlarge squares for your full-sized pattern to the size indicated.

To use the hand-enlargement method called transposing, you'll need cross-section graph paper (the kind with heavier lines marking off each square inch), a ruler, an eraser, and a soft-lead pencil. (If graph paper isn't available, make your own by dividing plain paper into the specified-size squares.)

Begin by marking off on your grid paper the same number of squares as indicated on the pattern grid. Next, number each vertical and horizontal grid line in the pattern. Then, number the corresponding grid lines on your graph paper the same way.

Start your pattern enlargement by finding a square on your graph paper that matches the same square on the original gridded pattern. Mark the graph paper grid square with a pencil dot in the same comparative place where a design line intersects a grid line on the original. Work only one square at a time. Continue to neighboring squares, marking each in the same way where a design line intersects a grid line.

To avoid discovering any mistakes too late, mark only part of the design, then stop and join the dots with a pencil line. Try to reproduce the original contours as accurately as possible. For more precision, draw all of the straight lines first; then add the curved and angled lines. Once you have transposed part of the design, finish marking the rest of the squares and join those dots in the same way.

Sometimes, you'll only have a *half-pattern* to use. To duplicate a full-sized half-pattern, copy the original with a soft-lead pencil on tracing paper. Next, flip your traced pattern over and place it pencil-lines-down onto one half of the board. After aligning the pattern for position, go over the pattern lines with your pencil to imprint it on the board. Then, flop the pattern onto the second half of the board and again retrace the pattern to imprint it. This method proves faster than copying with carbon paper and doesn't mark up the original pattern.

Using a copier to enlarge a gridded pattern

A photocopier with enlargement capability enlarges a gridded pattern faster than transposing. (Even a copier can be a little inaccurate, though, so always check your results with a ruler.)

To find out the enlargement percentage you'll need, use a pocket calculator to divide the scale square size (1") by the actual size of a gridded pattern square (for example, ½"). Your resulting enlargement will need to be 200% of the original.

However, most photocopiers do not enlarge at 200%. The copier you use may only have an enlargement limit of 150%. If this is the case, make a first enlargement of the original at 150%. Next, divide your desired final enlargement percentage (200) by 150. Your answer will be 133.

Then set the photocopier at 133%, and make a second enlargement of your first copy (which was made at 150%), and you'll end up with a pattern that is 200% larger than the gridded pattern. Check the final pattern with a ruler to make sure it is sized correctly. For example, an enlarged square on a 1" grid pattern needs to be exactly 1", not ⅞" or 1¹⁄₁₆". If it isn't, adjust the copier up or down a percentage or two, as necessary, until you end up with a pattern that is the correct size.